T0248457

GETTING TO RESILIENT MODE

TARIQ CHAUHAN

GETTING TO RESILIENT MODE

Finding the Path to Success Even When
the Odds Are Stacked Against You

Forbes | Books

Published by Forbes Books, Charleston, South Carolina.
Member of Advantage Media.

Forbes Books is a registered trademark, and the Forbes Books colophon is a trademark of Forbes Media, LLC.

Printed in the United States of America.

10 9 8 7 6 5 4 3 2 1

ISBN: 9798887501291 (Hardcover)
ISBN: 9798887501307 (eBook)

LCCN: 2022921812

Cover design by Megan Elger.
Layout design by David Taylor.

This custom publication is intended to provide accurate information and the opinions of the author in regard to the subject matter covered. It is sold with the understanding that the publisher, Forbes Books, is not engaged in rendering legal, financial, or professional services of any kind. If legal advice or other expert assistance is required, the reader is advised to seek the services of a competent professional.

Since 1917, Forbes has remained steadfast in its mission to serve as the defining voice of entrepreneurial capitalism. Forbes Books, launched in 2016 through a partnership with Advantage Media, furthers that aim by helping business and thought leaders bring their stories, passion, and knowledge to the forefront in custom books. Opinions expressed by Forbes Books authors are their own. To be considered for publication, please visit **books.Forbes.com**.

I would like to make a special mention of a woman of substance, my wife, Lovita. Without her by my side, I don't know if I would have had the strength to weather the storms, as well as not be swept away by the successes. Of course, the most beautiful gifts she has given me are my daughters, Nyla and Nada. Both girls have been my strongest supporters, given me my most honest critiques, and have taught me what resilience means.

With love, Tariq

CONTENTS

INTRODUCTION

*I stand at the end of no tradition; I may,
perhaps, stand at the beginning of one.*

—AYN RAND

This book is a true reflection of my introspection about the errors I made in life and the learnings therein. It brings in discourses and influences of some extraordinary people who touched my life. It encapsulates and summarizes all the learnings of my journey that I recall, in pursuit of making an impact. I have tried to bring my insight to various facets of my roller-coaster ride of highs and lows. I have also tried to explain the context of many business and professional challenges I faced and dealt with, especially the lessons learned from my lows. I had many brushes with the brute and harsh realities of life in my eventful life. Whatever I have written in this book is based on my honest introspection from confessions that gave me sense and wisdom. For me, undertaking business challenges was not part of an ambitious zeal alone but was also for my own pursuit of relevance, where impact mattered, with the sky as the limit. As a serial entrepreneur, I undertook numerous ambitious projects where I did go wrong, making fatal errors with many in managing business.

In this book, I concentrate on the lessons learned from my mistakes. About my long list of failures, from going broke with bankruptcy agencies knocking on my door, walking out of a partnership with nothing in hand, to venturing into multiple start-ups with zero capital—from these mistakes, I learned a great deal to tell others.

> I do not relent under any pressure and never let negativity cross my path.

On the personal front too, I went through a lot that shaped my resilient character. With my diagnosis of cancer, dealing with personal finance traumas after my business disasters, and struggling with an emotional family exigency having to do with one of my beloved children, I managed to keep my head on my shoulders, gaining some extraordinary life lessons. My relationships with my family and friends were an impeccable source of inspiration and emotional support that kept me intact and from breaking down during my turbulent times. I do not relent under any pressure and never let negativity cross my path. I must admit that my real-life encounters and brushes with crises gifted me with some deep insights that truly enriched my life, and these are the influences and learnings that I want to offer to my readers with this book.

My upbringing and values emboldened my strong sense of ethics and guided me to employ a purity of mind and morality in dealing with people. These attributes helped me in my sense of judging people and taught me how to *separate the men from the boys*. I never took people at face value, but my inquisitive nature and curiosity have always prompted me to look beyond the character to seek truth and see what lies within. As a keen observer, I always use my farsightedness and foresight to apply diligence, and you will notice this across my work in the book.

From the very early days, I would take whatever was given to me on an ownership basis and never shirk the accountability. These profound exposures helped me to gain deep insights into people and human behaviors. My troubles and that journey of fighting those crises actually shaped my life, as they do with all of us. These crises greatly influenced me and helped me to build a resilient character, and my thoughts in this book reflect those realities of life that I experienced. The pains and gains of my life are well articulated in the form of reference to context and are factored therein in various chapters.

My early years of life gave me immense exposure to wide shades of diversity in terms of culture, politics, and facts of life. Brought up in a small town and in a large family, I was able to develop a deep understanding of relationships, social dealings, behaviors, and cultural sensitivities. All these perspectives ultimately shaped my thoughts and are reflected in the people management section of the book. I lived in mixed cultures, small cities, and villages and traveled extensively between childhood and adolescence.

I was only sixteen when I represented my country in the World Festival of Youth and Students in the Soviet Union, and from then on I have been a "man on wheels," always in motion. With an extensive travel history, accumulating millions of travel miles, I am indeed a globe-trotter, having traveled to more than ninety countries. I have spent over five years of my life span in hotels, on flights, and in airports. These journeys have helped me gain deep insights into their history and culture. Working in big cities such as New York, London, Mumbai, and Hong Kong has also added to my knowledge of doing business in cross-border environments. The sights and sounds of the cities and countries I traveled to and worked in gave me an extensive perspective of what diversity means from people's varied cultural viewpoints. Be it the city's cosmopolitan character, the cultural fabric, or social behaviors, these journeys greatly influenced my exposure in context to my social awareness and work dealing with people, where sensitivity rules in managing people and their expectations.

I have tried my best in this book to connect to all those I view as my target readers, who can apply my learnings to their own insights when experiencing hardships. I am sure these readers will find opportunities to resonate with my experiences, as well as use these perspectives to manage their challenges and triumphs.

My chapter on leadership touches upon many facets and fundamentally focuses on my mantra of earning respect rather than demanding it, with the focus of embodying the values of a leader. I worked to ensure that people understand the true role of leadership, where they "walk the talk," and also that driving impact is the only measure of success. It's not just about benchmarks and the bottom line. In various articles I wrote about my belief that leaders must possess a passionate soul and have compassion for their workers. These qualities are known to drive the larger good of people, achieving holistic development for all stakeholders, and are much more valuable than self-obsessed leadership.

In my chapter on creating a people's organization that always puts people first, I have elaborated on multiple case studies of leadership building trust with the workforce by their strong engagement in the organizational mainstream through feedback, transparency, and effective performance management criteria. I also referred to driving higher self-actualization for employees, especially those on the bottom cadre. There are references to multiple aspects of *people-first approaches* in the chapters dedicated to people management.

The book has also covered many aspects of commercial prudence with chapters on the integrity of accounting practices, the role of banking and bankers' apathy, and the importance of business finance beyond accounting and bookkeeping.

There are also specific chapters where I deal with the world of governance and compliance. And here I show how, with the evolution of compliance, key lessons can be lost in translation, undermining their fundamental purpose.

PEOPLE

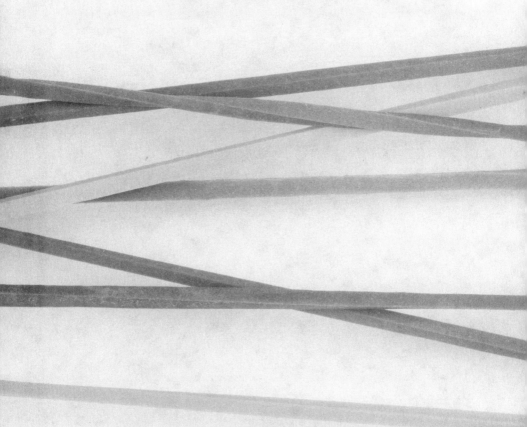

1. LEADERSHIP

Until I was in my midforties, I must confess it was mainly fame, an extravagant lifestyle, the excitement of conducting business, and creating business scalability that mattered most to me. I seldom ever applied my thoughts to my personal leadership style or considered my impact on my stakeholders. I had been part of a family where we shared values and common world perspectives. But even so, we always guarded our own individuality. My relationship with my daughters follows that tradition, as it is not just about doting on each other but much more a case of expressing mutual respect for each other. They help me to deeply introspect when I am wrong, whether it has to do with my dealings with people or my relationship with my wife. They also consult with me about their own moves and allow me to advise them as well. I must state that I remain under their close scrutiny and am always mindful of my actions at all times.

This change in direction began one morning after a conversation with my daughter, who wanted me to pursue making an *impact* on the world rather than just power, money, or fame. But actually it was later in my life when I realized the meaning of *impact* and why it matters for people leading change, who are responsible for delivering results. It began with my journey at EFS, when I began to measure the outcome of my efforts in terms of the impact I had on others, in life as well as in business. I was determined to drive my inputs toward ensuring measurable outcomes and worked to see those results benefit the stakeholders and touch the hearts of others. Only then did I start to see the impact that leaders could bring through their actions and the impact they could achieve in their leadership roles, which did not occur through just muted actions.

> Values were my strength from the very beginning, but in later years these became my guiding force to take on the full mettle of herculean challenges that came my way.

A compassionate heart, relentless action, a passionate soul, and self-reflection were the key attributes of leadership that I would seek to find in myself or those around me, who had what I consider to be "leadership souls."

Values were my strength from the very beginning, but in later years these became my guiding force to take on the full mettle of herculean challenges that came my way. I have consciously made them the cornerstone of my relationships, and in my business dealings these values helped set the guiding principles. I pride myself that my values have greatly influenced me across all facets: business, social, and family life. These have helped me shape some of the most extraordinary relationships in my personal life and business life. They have always guided me in my most trying times. People would often question my rigidity regarding my value-based feelings, as I would refuse business irrespective of its potential if it did not fit in with my value system. And in my personal life too, I would not lower my guard when it came to making any compromises that did not fit well with that value system.

Having been a strong believer in values, I always ensured that I and those who work with me minded our behavior carefully. During challenging times it is especially critical. Mature responses in our dealings with people matter, and throwing fits gains nothing. Our value system will always power our good conduct. It is a fact that people with sound values can better manage their most demanding times because their basic foundations are intact. For me, relationships with business associates, colleagues, and friends, in particular, can play a pivotal role in these turbulent times. In addition, these behaviors foster bonding between people, as colleagues, friends, or partners can bring help when needed.

Whether it was in regard to my personal life or business, I never gave in to negativity but maintained my perseverance to fight through, no matter what. In my struggles in business ventures, this attitude and perseverance helped me immensely to mitigate crises to seek positive results. These struggles gave me a profound understanding of business and the harsh realities of life and made me strong and able to be at ease when confronted with any adverse outcomes. I was mindful of taking those challenging times and the pains they caused as my learnings, *to rise above it all and not give in to negativity*. I became resilient in managing through the doldrums. Knowing that risk-taking is integral to doing business and always has its ups and downs, I prepared myself in advance for surprises. Over time, I could preempt these by applying the insight that I learned from my past. It did not mean that I was always good at it, but I learned to fortify and mitigate my ensuing risks through tough times.

A few salient aspects of my leadership journey at EFS were adopting the people-first approach and keeping an eye on business sustainability.

People, systems, and structure were the fundamental ethos guiding my journey at EFS. In my perpetual quest for creating impact in my life and my professional work, whether it was a task, job, or mission, team selection and its specific dynamics were always at the forefront of my mind to execute a task.

Team means people, and my basis for selecting a team and the people therein is always based upon the embodiment of values in all I do and incorporating the vital attributes of discipline, attitude, and commitment.

In order to build their *conviction to deliver results*, a good team effort and apt chemistry are needed.

With an eye on a shared vision, I ensured that team members saw engagements and accomplishments as opportunities for their professional development as well as their self-development. I prioritized forging alliances in most of my work, with colleagues or companies based on genuine partnerships with shared goals and values. I cobbled these alliances together all my life based on deep mutual respect and relationships to build conviction. I would go out of my way to focus on this prerequisite whenever building new teams or putting up a new project. I would ensure that the team understood that these accomplishments would have a definitive holistic impact, resulting in their own higher self-actualization.

I am proud of the relationships that I have built with my colleagues. In most team engagements, I make it a point to engage the team to first buy into my leadership through respect by virtue of my tangible contribution for the purpose at hand. I also see to it that the team has shared values and ownership in the mission by conviction and see this mission in alignment with their self-development goals. Besides these, it's also essential to view the benefits of the learnings resulting from the journey itself as life enriching. I have worked to make sure that all were made aware that these learnings were integral to their interests. I wanted to ensure that my colleagues were mindful of the understandings, not just the successes but also the failures, with deep introspections that would enable them to be resilient.

1.1. Personal Lifestyle and Behavioral Attributes

Discipline has been one of my greatest strengths, and this came as a distinct advantage in my rise up the corporate ladder. This shaped my personality and professional progress, which resulted in a higher level of work productivity as well as personal happiness.

Whether on a personal, family, or business level, the practice of discipline has achieved the respect and reputation I enjoy among my peers and staff. Adhering to the code of ethics and discipline has never posed a challenge or acted as a deterrent in achieving my goals. Although some regard these practices, such as punctuality, as utopian or a misplaced idealism, these are instead proud credentials that helped me to forge great alliances and lifelong relationships.

At work I was careful not to lower the bar, whether it had to do with my corporate attire, meeting schedules, or efficient organization of my office staff. There was zero tolerance. Cultural values required within the company included adherence to discipline. I was aware that self-discipline encompasses a much broader spectrum of personality attributes, including behavioral, and the company's hiring process now has multiple checks to ensure behavioral attributes align with our core values.

Personal discipline ensures that people can push forward, stay motivated, and take action, regardless of how they feel, physically or emotionally. Motivation and willpower contribute to it, as does persistence, the ability to follow through on your intentions, and, of course, hard work. In my life too, this was my most powerful tool to reinvent myself to rise to face the adversities I encountered. For example, during the 2008 economic crisis, I was concerned about my failing health as a diabetic patient. The crises wrecking my well-being could have had a lifelong impact with disastrous consequences. However, my lifestyle and self-discipline helped me to achieve a much-needed resilience.

Reflection Points

- Discipline and positivity have been the two most significant attributes that have guided me throughout my life journey. These important behaviors have helped me to navigate through the most challenging of times.

- Working always with these attributes in the forefront of my mind, I was able to maintain a mindful state that would allow me to rise above all adversity.

1.2. Demonstrating Ethical Leadership Is a Necessity

I have always held the fundamental belief that ethical leadership emanates from the values that one embodies each day. Values have always been my critical guiding principles for dealing with people. In this way, I can ensure that mutual respect, transparency, honesty, integrity, and fairness prevail to gain people's trust. In my company, my key focus has been to earn people's trust through my actions and their measured outcomes, not promises alone. As an example, at the beginning of the COVID-19 pandemic, with over 80 million job losses worldwide occurring in just a few months, at EFS I promised zero job losses to my strong contingent of a twenty-two-thousand-person workforce. By the year's end, there were 250 million job losses globally, but EFS had none.

Respect is another integral part of the value matrix that matters to me. One must not underestimate the importance of mutual respect in corporate environments. Indeed, every individual deserves respect, and no one, irrespective of their position, background, or class, can choose to take that away from anyone.

I believe that a CEO's real test lies in his or her role to engage and motivate the C suite to lead their teams. They must not operate as lone wolves but rather be seen as inspiring and leading the company, ensuring that their dedicated and inspired teams execute their plans and vision. A company's workforce needs much more than just the CEO though; they need the executive management to lead them on multiple fronts.

Of course, the CEO is the sole architect of the company's vision, but to carry out the vision, CEOs need their C-suite peers to fully engage and execute the agenda outlined in that vision. These members must take this as a mission-critical agenda that is encrypted in their hearts and souls and inspired by respect and faith in their leader and their leader's decisions. It must not be a case of just orders taken from the boss.

These executives are expected to be sharp executioners with a defined path and collective resolve, operating from a shared vision and values that the organization has adopted. Executive leadership cannot afford to deviate from the path set forth by their CEO but instead have to build workforce engagement and activism along those lines.

> Fulfilling a leadership role requires a commitment to cement the *vision*, based on strong values that are coshared and owned mutually by all.

Fulfilling a leadership role requires a commitment to cement the *vision*, based on strong values that are coshared and owned mutually by all. These values bind the team with a common resolve to succeed and enable them to effectively lead their teams and their colleagues.

During corporate conversations, certain instances will always come up where leadership will have disruptive behaviors. Leaders have to work hard to guard their composure in such situations. However tricky or explosive the mistake or problem may be, a calm and rational approach is fundamental to arrive at any meaningful resolution.

Often, specific correctional interactions that may be necessary between the boss and the subordinate will lead to aggressive postures. It is unwarranted and unnecessary, though it is true it seems to be a natural behavior for some in the corporate world. But these fracases or aggressive behaviors are unhealthy. Even when leaders must give challenges, comparisons, or corrections, these need to adhere to specific protocols, and deviating from that is a mistake that corporate cultures must protect against. Anger and aggression from a boss in dealing with his or her colleagues is not an option but rather an unnecessary evil. Respect, even in the face of disagreements, must be a value that all organizations are ready to stand upon and uphold.

The CEO needs to build a medium of engagement with C-suite colleagues or others, where corrective outcomes are sought without resorting to aggression or displaying loss of patience. Where mistakes are diagnosed, not dissected, the CEO can indeed express his disappointment with a tone of assertion but not a lack of respect. Unexpected results or bad outcomes do come under the scrutiny of bosses and do face the ire of leadership, but what matters most is the conduct of the CEO to manage these situations. While it may be frustrating, no positive results can be achieved through adverse reactions. Respect for the CEO increases among colleagues if they choose patience and determine correctional engagements with respect. This emboldens trust. However severe a bad business outcome may be, no amount of goodwill or intention is worthwhile if the leader does not align his communication with a basic code of respect that every individual needs. Leadership roles require not only clarity of purpose, a loftiness of vision, but also compassionate communication. It is a two-way process where respect is earned, not demanded.

This also applies to leadership roles where one has to be mindful of their communication with their colleagues. Even in the most challenging conversations, leaders must maintain their composure. One must seek a corrective approach to ensure positive outcomes. Punitive actions such as threatening job security, financial penalties, or any personal attacks will always be disastrous. Instead, more conciliatory tones of an impactful corrective process need to be outlined. Always take the opportunity to engage the proponent to know their mistake, to own it, and embark upon the correction process.

In my journey as the Group CEO, my engagement outcomes with my team have always been a critical area of focus. I address my weaknesses as well as work tirelessly to overcome every impediment that I have, in order to be a fair and compassionate boss.

I try to ensure that no one fears me. Often in the past, anger and intense reactions emerged out of my frustrations. I learned from these lapses and worked to make constructive changes in my own behavior. This has helped me see some great results.

There remains a lot of work in progress, but this process requires perpetual introspection to mend. This aspect is always on my list of habits to work on and improve.

I would summarize my leadership vision in the words of a great poet, Allama Iqbal, which greatly influenced me and explained the nine dimensions of ethical leadership: "The loftiness of vision, communication that touches the heart, passionate soul, truth, justice, courage, reflection, self-awareness, and relentless action."

In essence, I found my way by implementing these convictions to best execute my actions.

Reflection Points

- Having lived in the midst of a society with hypocritical and complex conventions, I have found it necessary to always keep my core values at the forefront. It's essential to ensure that all actions we take as leaders can be seen as aligned with the set of ethical values that we profess to follow.

- In pursuit of our goals and ambitions, we as leaders must remain mindful of our ethical values and commitments and show them clearly with every decision taken. Deviating from these can be disastrous for morale, as this will create a trust deficit with your stakeholders.

1.3. Altruism Must Not Just Be Professed but Practiced

Altruism for business leaders and companies is no longer just another attribute of good governance. It is a requirement to keep employees fully engaged and to help the organization realize its wider goals. One critical aspect of altruism is to demonstrate to your employees that the company stands for the holistic good of stakeholders, not just profits and management interests. CEO posturing and actions need to transcend beyond self-good and shareholders, and instead reach out to *all* stakeholders.

Conventional employee engagement methods are no longer sufficient to maintain a healthy connection between employees and the organization. More importantly, it must consist of definitive actions backed by *shared goals*. At EFS, we have tried our best to build trust in something very specific, and that is self-good and constant evolution. We have been attempting to align individual goals and ambitions to the shared organizational vision, where there is *a common good for all.*

While human resources (HR) teams can manage routine grievances and counseling needs, it is up to the bosses at every level to co-own this responsibility. It should not just be left to the human resources department to take on this responsibility. Still, the entire leadership quadrant must have the mettle to engage their teams to drive enterprise ownership. Team engagement is not just about work performance but also the need to adopt more inclusive participation where their development and happiness is the focal point and not just work-related key performance indicators (KPIs).

Building trust among colleagues is a requirement that all managers need to achieve. For an employee to have faith in their bosses, the company's strategy and values need to be aligned with the principles of altruism. It is not just for the CEO to adopt altruism—the company as a whole needs to embrace it.

In any organization, managers must rise to be both mentors and guides. They have to adapt themselves through continued self-development of the relevant capabilities and personality traits that this role demands.

To achieve such a stature, the executives in these positions have to connect with employees in a more personal way. The staff must be able to differentiate their manager from that of a preacher to one who "walks the talk." All employees must be able to seek counsel from their superiors and not fear any reprisals from disclosures they might make.

As a CEO, I knew I needed to lead with altruism from the top. I developed multiple avenues to connect with my employees, especially with the frontline workers, where building trust was paramount to strengthening altruism's pillars. In their moment of earnest need, I prioritized compassion over red tape. I made sure I could make decisions and drive impact through my related actions, such as guaranteeing 100 percent job safety, education for needy and deserving children, funding for elderly parents, and assisting any employee with their dire needs. Above all, I ensured that I led an organization where compassion with merits is embedded in the organization's mainstream and prioritized.

Bosses need to strengthen their core values to be able to demonstrate the stature of a real leader. There are salient approaches that differentiate leaders from followers, not just through overtures such as getting to know employees by name but in knowing everything about the employees, including their health, family, and even finances. No, this is not an indulgence but a much-needed effort often ignored by leaders and organizations.

It is equally essential that organizational values concerning leadership—especially those that focus on the inclusivity element—are retained while the company is continually transforming. The communication strategy from the board has to be emphatic to ensure that all policies are well articulated and *understood across all levels.*

A company must build an effective communication strategy based on inclusivity and not just media showcasing. It must focus not only on an external audience to support the brand but also on its internal channels to boost employee engagement. All developments such as board changes, any management restructuring, acquisitions, and outstanding contributions of unsung heroes must be highlighted across the organization.

A pressing need is to initiate employee engagement for organizations with a sizeable blue-collar population. To gain their trust is of utmost importance, as their self-actualization goals are quite different and complex, with elements that can differ from the white-collar staff.

Their concerns about living conditions, family connectivity, and finances are paramount to building an apt engagement strategy. Encouraging health and well-being awareness as well as supporting financial planning and discipline among less-privileged employees are initiatives that can significantly influence employees' engagement and motivation.

Reflection Points

- I was aware that to achieve the true impact of my altruistic beliefs throughout my career, I had to go the extra mile by building a bond of trust with my employees where they could see me "walking my talk." In this context, I ensured my actions were well communicated, understood by all stakeholders, and informed of the benefits of those actions that would transform their lives.

- I was very emphatic in driving my ideology that employees' personal and professional good will eventually increase the organization's larger good. I focused on engaging people in their personal and professional development and interwound the organization to build a bond of trust with employees to achieve their holistic good.

1.4. Diversity and Inclusion Are Business Sustainability Needs

Diversity and inclusivity are evolving considerations that matter in both public and work life. In recent years they have gained traction, but a lot still needs to be done. Evolving perspectives need to feed into a sustainable movement with more emphatic milestones. Prior to EFS, it never occurred to me that this was such an important business sustainability requirement to consider. With so many nationalities and ethnic groups across so many economic classes, I realized the need. At EFS, bringing women to the forefront in an industry such as facilities management was challenging. Being a fieldwork-centric industry with certain innate hardships and perceptions, it was a daunting task to get women on board with full force. To make it happen, we realized that our leadership had to champion this initiative by paving the way for opportunities that would act as a launchpad for a far-reaching impact on female empowerment.

We realized that no organization can sustain growth and prosper without having an ecosystem and a fundamental value system for inclusivity. So we built a holistic organization, meeting the prerequisites to enable women to rise in their careers and excel. Women now make up almost a third of our C-suite leadership team and another 25 percent of the workforce in the United Arab Emirates (UAE). They spearhead vital business functions and have helped transform the company. We ensure there is a reflection of opportunities and fairness for all women, be they engineers, resident technicians, housekeeping staff, or executives.

Whether in regard to personal, family, community, business, or public concerns, inclusion matters. It goes a long way for those in pursuit of a value-based journey that encompasses life at home, at work, and in society itself. People need to understand the impact reflecting upon their core values will have on all other aspects of their lives and how they can fulfill their moral and ethical challenges beyond their faith, thereby cutting across race, religion, or gender.

Inclusion is fundamental to the ethos of any civil society and integral to the principles of most religions. Due to a lack of insight and misconceived perceptions, this remains a hotly debated issue. Its pros and cons are always under scrutiny, and unfortunately its merits are intensely contested by many. These preconceived apprehensions about inclusion must be examined for viability. The politics of the day are now helping to ensure that these biases and discrimination will be addressed.

Inclusivity assures the greater good for all, while it also aims to focus on the weaker sections of the workforce to ensure that they get a level playing field as well as to offer adequate resources for those workers to enable them to integrate into other areas of the workplace. Inclusivity is not about taking anything away from anyone. It is to engage the privileged in helping the vulnerable sections of the workforce to further elevate social and economic order. This narrative, at times, becomes a challenge for some, with inclusivity often wrongly perceived as a threat to those with privileges, who worry that these privileges may be taken away or that they may be asked to share them with others.

For a sustainable social order, coherence is a fundamental need in each walk of life to ensure equal opportunities, fairness, justice, and trust. Inclusivity, in essence, eradicates biases and discrimination and promotes a consciousness of *coherence*. For the development of society or the workplace, all prejudices and frontiers of race, religion, gender, or economic class must go. Society and the world at large need inclusion to take away deep-rooted biases and create balance. Inclusion aims to engage with the haves to co-own their principles and work to bring equal opportunities for the have-nots.

Diversity is critical to further the desired impact of inclusivity. In any civil society, diversity is essential in terms of the participation or representation of all classes. Ethnic, religious, gender, and cultural diversity ensure that all coexist. In the business world too, inclusivity and diversity are the essential drivers. Principal business segments, such as people and strategy, are critical inclusivity considerations that shape business continuity and performance outcome.

Inclusivity assures that people from different ethnicities, nationalities, religions, and cultures quickly learn to *coexist despite their diverse backgrounds*. It helps to elevate people to excel and, often, to outperform. As part of the inclusion agenda, diversity ensures that ethnic, cultural, and religious groups are more tolerant, risk savvy, and outgoing in their domains.

Inclusion in the workplace puts the onus on the company's policies, values, and culture. The organization's values act as the custodian of inclusion, and these set its guiding principles, from systems to the management of the human workforce across all the functional domains of the business.

Diversity will ensure a reasonable representation of all classes incorporating nationality, gender, and ethnicity. In contrast, compassion will ensure that weaker sections and their interests are not overlooked. Gender equality will ease the way for women to continue to succeed and work seamlessly in all departments. Data and research prove that diversity and inclusion assure greater organizational sustainability and economic leverage.

We tirelessly worked on the inclusion aspect and introduced a series of measures to increase employee engagement in the organization. These measures included a SpeakOut platform, for people to raise their grievances and suggestions to the highest level, and the introduction of Madad, to help employees instantly reach out to the company with all their feedback and suggestions. This resulted in achieving over 95 percent engagement levels. The launch of the Centurion Club as the reward and recognition program resulted in an over 15 percent progression between housekeeping and technical jobs. Over the last ten years, I have ensured that 10 percent of the company's cost is dedicated to frontline welfare, which includes the well-being and learning and development of our employees, a rare gesture in an industry where single-digit margin rules are a common sight, and such high allocations are seldom to be seen.

Additionally, the diversity principle was applied as a rule of thumb in all our recruitment drives with a critical mix of nationality, gender, language, religion, and ethnic background. Today, the company represents over thirty-five nationalities and has a fair representation of males and females in its frontline job positions. This shift has produced significant positive results across the board.

Reflection Points

- The wisdom gained from research demands that organizations ensure diversity by including different interest groups, religions, castes, and social classes to build a robust and tolerant culture.

- Diversity and inclusion have evolved as a necessity to create an environment where equality begins to flourish and biases are removed.

- Leaders must work tirelessly to create this just and fair environment in their organizations.

1.5. Life 101: Transforming Mistakes into Success

There have been prolonged public debates and deliberations on how to introspect when things go wrong. Now, professionals, entrepreneurs, and people are starting to use 360° approaches while looking back to reexamine what lessons can be learned. These learnings are vital as they ultimately help also in shaping a better future. A definitive transformation is happening in people's mindsets as more executives are starting to admit their mistakes and not just "blaming it on Rio."

We all have regrets in our life, but how often do we analyze their outcomes and apply these learnings? We seldom take the blame, as instead we will often rush to blame the circumstances. We must realize that a thorough individual analysis and an ability to be critical are necessary to understand lessons learned from our failures. It will accomplish nothing if we accept failures without applying logic to the reasons for our failings. It is not useful to simply blame the circumstances. Everyone must work to understand their own constraints and how they contributed to mistakes that led to adverse outcomes.

The "blame it on Rio" syndrome of success and failure is part of life. Therefore, one must react calmly in context to failures while looking back on what went wrong. In any situation, ranging from marital discord to professional life woes or business turbulence, introspection is indeed a herculean challenge, as we do not always want to admit our failings. But to not do so is to risk disaster.

Instead of looking at ourselves, we often choose to blame everything else. No matter what the situation may be, people will hold circumstances and/or others to be responsible for failures without being able to see the actual cause. For instance, in marital problems, those circumstances could include the spouse, her/his siblings, family financial needs, health, or work pressure.

In our professional life, career, and job challenges, poor relationships with peers and demanding bosses are the usual suspects. In business the blame could be market conditions, capital woes, cash flow, partner relations, and shareholders. We must truly work to analyze any shortcomings that might have led to an unwished-for debacle.

For instance, in the case of marital discord, we are quick to blame the spouse for all ills. But we hardly look within ourselves to gauge whether it is our own shortcomings that are helping to create the rift. We blame compatibility. But it may have to do with personality issues that we all need to improve and work on.

The same is true regarding our professional life, where we end up with many misguided conclusions without looking closely at ourselves. Not admitting to your mistakes is one colossal mistake that people often make. It is noteworthy that in my twenty-seven years of professional life, most people who I have interviewed for work were somehow emphatic that their adverse occupational outcomes were due to a series of events or circumstances rather than their own professional errors or career miscalculations. Professionals must realize that making mistakes is something we all experience, and with introspection it can be the best way to learn and move forward with more success in the future.

This is why psychometric evaluations are now used, so that professionals can map their capabilities and constructively address their self-introspections while dealing with their peers and bosses.

In most organizations, an individual's performance is based on self-capability and the ability to influence his or her peers to maximize the team output. In this scenario, a candid intrapersonal skill is needed to ensure a reliable result as well as to build a healthy relationship with peers. The same could be said regarding one's relationship with the boss, where it could either be your intrapersonal skills that are in play or fitting in with the boss's preferences in regard to his or her subordinate's skill set.

Every boss has some expectations for the employees in regard to the key performance indicators. Therefore, it is a must that employees align their strengths and weaknesses to meet their KPIs to deter any personal or unambiguous conclusions. Uncertainty in these situations often results in either affecting one's job satisfaction or making unnecessary career moves.

The usual reasons cited for business failures include adverse capital market conditions, economic growth whirlwinds, boardroom squabbles, and lack of strategic direction, cash flow, capitalization issues, and shareholders' expectations. I do concur that these are the factors that might influence a good business, but at the same time I believe that, with prudent business management skills, these risks can easily be mitigated, and the enterprise can also easily be safeguarded. Every competent CEO must foresee this as a critical business prerequisite and must embolden risk management at all times to deter any unnecessary risks. In the absence of adequate risk management strategy, risks such as market conditions, client defaults, etc. can negate the performance and lead to failure.

Success in business is not an option; it's a requirement. Therefore, business leaders and CEOs, rather than contemplating about a likely collapse or damage control strategies, must concentrate on building *sustainability*. How often does a CEO stand up to make a confession about their failures but instead shrouds these by connecting their outcomes to circumstances that they judge to be outside of their control? We have seldom seen business leaders applying those learnings they have gained from their errors. They are either not honest or are overwhelmed by the negativity, and they try to neutralize the situation by holding these external factors as being responsible. CEOs as leaders need to rise against all the odds. It does not suit them to blame their failure on others or circumstances. Instead, they should work to find answers to their self-failings to enable them to move forward, as they are part of a chosen few, being appointed, empowered, and expected to build a sustainable enterprise.

While we sincerely wish to engage in introspection about our lives, we should take care to apply the right learnings from our failings.

This exercise of inner soul-searching shows us the much-needed direction that we usually look for in turbulent times. It is true that circumstances and situations do influence outcomes, but this is where our upbringing, values, and professional skills come in handy. Also, our other attributes, such as strategy, emotional intelligence, and commercial prudence, play a pivotal role in mitigating all the risks that led to unfortunate events. One more vital truth is the state of mind and much-needed positivity for a candid assessment of one's personalized evaluation. A sound state of mind can neutralize all negative elements as well as ensure a much-needed ecosystem for the desired soul-searching exercise. However, certain counseling aids can also be useful. Activities such as counseling and psychometric tests show the way for people to learn how to activate their self-corrective mechanism and embolden their resolve to change for the better.

Reflection Points

- The most significant gift I achieved from the low points of my life was my resilient mode, where I did not dwell on my failures but applied deep introspection from the lessons learned. This is an achievable goal for any leader who aspires to excellence.

- I have always worked to correct my path, using my learning to rise above my previous mistakes. This is the most important lesson of resilience, one that every leader must learn.

1.6. Business Leadership—the Predicament between Saving the Bottom Line and Retaining Jobs

The COVID-19 pandemic was a litmus test for CEOs on how to navigate their enterprise against its challenges. The whole world was within the epicenter of this calamity, ill-prepared, grappling to deal with its horrendous impact, and jostling to respond. This crisis has brought many industries to their knees. It is testing the resilience of all businesses, not only those in survival mode. Even industries such as food and medical supplies, which are in upswing mode due to a spurt in demand, have challenges with production and supply chain woes. Business is stranded, struggling to cope with the effects of the pandemic.

No report or analysis has been able to assess its real impact, with perhaps the worst yet to come. There are clear signs of severe financial fatigue, in particular firms and industries. SMEs, in particular, are profusely bleeding. Many businesses are in ventilator mode, and nothing seems inevitable. It is on every CEO's agenda to contain the damage and its snowballing effect on revenues, cost overruns, and cash flow. Most are concentrating on cost purges and contemplating strategies on how to mitigate these challenges. Job cuts are emerging as a measure being taken by many companies to limit their impact.

The International Labor Organization has forecasted over 195 million job losses globally amid the COVID-19 crisis, with companies across the globe announcing pay cuts and layoffs. Of the many challenges that corporate leadership has had to deal with in this crisis, from market assessment to business sustainability aspects, maintaining the trust of the people working in the organization is quintessential.

Business leaders need to evolve by taking decisive and emphatic postures to steer companies out of this whirlpool. The balancing act required to keep a company afloat between business prudence and employee retention is a lifetime challenge for any ship captain who must somehow keep afloat in unchartered waters while also protecting everyone on board.

Indeed, this is what most CEOs are facing today. The current fear syndrome, job insecurity, and looming slowdown are all playing havoc with people's minds. It is a daunting task these days to keep staff motivated, even for stable companies, as fears of job security are always on people's minds. Most employees know if the going gets tough, austerity measures, including job losses, might come into play. Keeping employees engaged in such conditions is a challenging task. For a business to navigate out of any turbulence, it is imperative to take the workforce on board with good communication. Leaders have to go the extra mile to bring everyone into their confidence with the greatest of respect, especially those who must leave the company.

Corporate leaders in these testing times need to display their convictions with deep foresight and confidence that can motivate and engage people. In any business, employee happiness is the foremost business driver. Cost optimization and efficiency can serve to minimize the impact and avoid the drastic steps of cutting jobs whenever possible. In any business, a sustainable business model needs to be planned for contingencies. Diversification of revenue models and putting sufficient risk mitigation strategies in place are important tools. For example, at EFS, we were able to add new service lines and reskill some of our workforce to meet new service requirements during the COVID-19 onset. This was not easy. It was led by an early identification of the upcoming market demand. We saw the rising need for disinfection services, and we deployed all resources to license, train, and educate our employees on how to deliver these services. The new service line allowed us to retain our employees and contribute additional profits to the business, which allowed us to further develop the business through the turbulent period that followed. While this may not be an example that is applicable to all businesses, there are many businesses that evolved during the same period as well by seeking out new opportunities. Many businesses developed an online presence with free delivery options, and some offered new home-based services, while others expanded service offerings via digital platforms. More infrastructure-based services suffered, such as airlines. In many instances, there were no alternative service arrangements that could have been offered, or costs that could have been reviewed, to allow for staff to be retained. It is a business case that will remain open for years to discuss as we continue to see warnings of increased impacts from unfortunate global events such as pandemics and global warming.

Often, many businesses can avoid a resource purge with other innovative strategies. Letting people go is counterproductive in people-centric businesses, especially in a crisis where human resources are the key to any revival plans and should always be the last option.

Often, entrepreneurs and corporate leaders argue that saving jobs is not their responsibility, as this mantra interferes with the principles of entrepreneurship. I would say that while the government has its obligations to its people, business leaders must also not shy away from creating and protecting jobs as part of their social responsibility.

If cutting the workforce is a necessity, then adherence to due sensitivity is needed. However, this should always be the last resort. To cut jobs is easy, but it has a far-reaching effect and leaves long-lasting scars on the organization and the people.

Reflection Points

- CEOs must exhaust every other viable option to save jobs and avoid demoralizing people by making job cuts, which usually proves counterproductive.

- When in crisis mode, employee retention is the most significant driver to ensure effective business restitution or revival.

1.7. A Passionate Soul and Relentless Action

I was always viewed as being a passionate soul by everyone I ever met and interacted with. Because of my passion, there was never a dull moment in my life. It was always a relentless drive with a pursuit for relevance. Pursuing action, seeking impact, and challenging the status quo constitutes the fervor of my life. My teachers used to get frustrated with my barrage of questions in class, as I would never stop with my continuous push for actions with outcomes. *I would simply never give up.*

Some people say that a leader's spirit must be fired with zeal. For me, passion for achieving my objectives was never an option but a foregone conclusion. It was always in abundance with a single-minded determination to fire my underlying decisions. I was never held up by paralysis and planning in my decision-making. My actions emanate from a passion fired by faith in people's perceived goodness, and faith that good would eventually prevail upon evil. Difficulties, obstacles, hindrances, and barriers never discouraged me but rather firmed my resolve.

This passion gave me the intellectual guidance and ability to mobilize the people I needed. Passion provides the compass that continually gives direction toward the desired destination and allows for countless opportunities to recoup and recover from setbacks and circumnavigate around insurmountable obstacles.

Leadership is not only about having lofty visions; it is about sustained effort and relentless actions in the face of adversity. The dogged determination of a leader resembles the rapids that are formed with a single trickle of water dropping from a glacier, which then combines together with other trickles to form a small stream, which in turn combines with other such streams to form a river with white water rapids roaring down the slopes of mountains and valleys, creating ravines and paths through the gigantic rocks that impede their way.

Whenever these rivers flow down from rocky mountainous slopes into the plains, they transform from a thunderous torrent to a mellifluously gentle stream. Similarly, the leader marches with his or her followers, who keep on joining together with other converts, and with synergy he or she leads them stridently in the face of opposition. An unassailable optimism guides this movement of a leader toward the goal and helps in overcoming each seemingly insurmountable barrier.

Reflection Points

- Leaders must possess a passionate soul and have compassion for their workers.

- These qualities drive the larger good of the people, achieve holistic development for all stakeholders, and are much more valuable than self-obsessed leadership.

1.8. Truth and Fairness Must Prevail

An organizational value system must always safeguard its goals and objectives, and it also assures that trust prevails in the organizational bloodstream.

Truth and fairness are the essential characteristics of a human relationship. In the case of a business or organization, leadership needs to rise to the challenge and guarantee that the organization is seen as fair and transparent, a place where truthfulness rules. This is a basic necessity to instill confidence in people in the organization, which requires transparency and truth, especially for the leaders and their managers. They must not only be professing it but practicing it. This should not be about tokenism but rather a way for them to create a culture that embeds the principle of truthfulness.

All stakeholders must ensure consistency in the way they communicate, so that they are seen to be fair in all their actions without any bias. Company communication on critical decisions is often lost in translation and seemingly inconsistent with its articulated vision; it is vital to be careful not to show inconsistencies.

At EFS, I was especially careful in this context. In spite of building a solid bond of trust with people, I was highly aware of the need to go back to people and discuss and decode our messages and rationale to ensure full understanding for all. I knew if we didn't reach out, our efforts would be in vain.

Fairness is another attribute of a leader to sustain impact. Leaders cannot sustain their impact if they are not seen as being fair in dealing with people or businesses. For me, too, in building EFS, a people-first organization, it was my utmost priority that all view my actions and decisions as fair and completely transparent.

I would go the extra mile to ensure effective communication regarding all my strategies, decisions, and actions so that everyone could understand my rationale. I worked to build a bond with my employees and stakeholders where trust and transparency were the fundamental drivers.

Reflection Points

- A leader's biggest asset is the trust that they have gained with the people who work in the organization.

- It is critical that people see the leader as fair and transparent in his or her actions and decisions. The leader must enable trust and effectively communicate the reasons for his or her decisions at all times.

- Justice and fairness are what differentiate an ethical leader from an opportunistic leader.

1.9. A Leader's Vision Must Empower All Stakeholders

I was always mindful that my grand vision of building a billion-dollar organization needed to be shared by all to be successful, where my team, my family, and my shareholders all could come together. I wanted to build an organization where a billion-dollar objective was not only its valuation but also one that incorporated the holistic good of all stakeholders, including our clients. I knew that I could create a powerful bond with stakeholders if the vision was clearly articulated. That vision would give our employees not just the security of a job but opportunities to grow, learn, and be a part of an institution that is a rising star with a long-standing sustainability. This loftiness of vision also helps build a team of great C-suite executives as future leaders, who only wish to align with ambitious projects and organizations that keep an eye on the big picture. Success in leadership is not only about having lofty visions, but it is also about sustained effort and relentless actions, never giving up no matter what problems might present themselves.

Reflection Points

- Companies and management must ensure that the vision statement has an aspiring zeal and percolates down across the entire organization.

- The statement itself must have impact, have clarity about the company's direction, and offer holistic growth and prosperity for all.

1.10. Leaders and Managers Must Ensure Communication That Touches the Heart

The second essential competency of the leader is the ability to touch the hearts and minds of the people. This can only happen if your message is coming out from the depth of your heart. Your intention should be infused with the kind of sincerity and selflessness that will only come from the purity of your purpose. The purpose should be to enable the visions of the followers and not to achieve a self-focused agenda.

This communication stands in stark contrast to the manipulative agenda of "behavioral change" often taught in courses of organizational behavior, which emphasize "conditioning" through extrinsic motivators of carrot-and-stick to increase the equity value of organizational shareholders! This contrast represents the essential difference between leadership and management. The inability of a leader's communication to address the hearts of the followers creates mistrust and disillusionment and eventually leads to their estrangement.

Communication is an essential lever of any business engagement, though it has often missed its true impact by getting lost in translation. In the context of contract management especially, effective communication holds the key to success. It ensures ease in managing contract deliverables, from service delivery to seamless client engagement and desired transparency. The defined communication protocol is thus an essential requirement for an engagement that builds trust and transparency, and it must be put in place along with the contract setup stage.

Effective communication encompasses a verbal, written, and process-driven communication framework with clearly laid out standards and operating procedures.

A great proficiency in oral and written communication does not necessarily achieve the requisite communication standards. This requires a defined communication protocol or framework in line with the contractual needs. Although "I said," or "she said," or "I have sent the mail," or other informal communications are considered by many as adequate, these do not meet the necessary standards. Effective communication requires good information management to keep everyone in the loop with defined action points, and the transmission must be closed with action items acknowledged or agreed upon.

Good process-driven communication is necessary with a result-oriented approach emphasizing effectiveness, transparency, timeliness, and situational needs. Therefore, it is essential that contract personnel strictly adhere to a protocol that requires more than written and verbal communication skills. A suitable protocol needs role-based skills, defined engagement guidelines, and an escalation matrix with each process-related defined touchpoint. The protocol should have a clearly defined process for communication under normal day-to-day operations with a well-defined engagement matrix and escalation matrix for crisis management.

People often fail to deal with exigencies as their communication during a crisis goes awry. Disaster management needs very elaborate crisis communications protocols. Therefore, it is imperative to draw a line between routine communications and crisis communications. In specific regard to crisis contacts, besides adhering to given operating procedures as laid out in the protocol, it is necessary to use tactical communication effectively.

How to deliver bad news or avoid miscommunication, or to control overzealous communiques when dealing in contingency environments, are instances where tactical communication plays a key role, and it should be addressed in the data-driven world of today. The ensuing time pressures often cause people to disseminate information that may be inaccurate or incomplete. The process should thus outline clear guidelines by adhering to the integrated management best practices.

Depending on each person's role, the requisite communication competence should be defined. For example, the ground-level workforce needs only basic speaking and writing skills. In the project leadership quadrant, whether it has to do with a supervisor, manager, or general manager, each level requires specific skills for effective communications management. For example, people in the supervision tier are supposed to manage their staff, and in this instance practical verbal communication matters more than written communication. However, for the managerial roles, written and oral proficiency to ensure tactical communications are critical. In client engagements, besides oral and verbal language, proficiency should be in role-centric communication competency.

My emphasis on process-driven communication refers to defined points relating to service delivery, client engagement, and escalation and also toward crisis management. Technology, up to an extent, can provide some direction. But it is the company protocols that should clearly define the process-driven communication touchpoints.

In my twenty-five years as a CEO, I have seen how bad communication negatively impacts the business, be it in client engagements or in internal organizational dealings. Due to poor communication, I refer to this common problem as an example of being "lost in translation." Indeed, the inability to derive the desired impact as well as receiving strong pushback from clients are the expected outcomes when failing to communicate effectively. Industry professionals need to master the art of effective communication, as this alone can win most battles.

Reflection Points

- Leaders must make an effort to touch people's hearts. This can only happen if they build deep commitment and conviction that is driven by their own hearts.

- Their intention should demonstrate sincerity and selflessness, ensuring a purity of purpose that will create trust.

- The purpose should not have a self-driven agenda, and the communication therein must convey the spirit of purpose that offers compassion and a holistic good for all.

1.11. Courage Helps Manage Business Risks

Courage requires owning up to decisions and moving forward despite the risk. It is often what it takes to stand up to and withstand the pressures and overcome fears, apprehensions, and uncertainties. It certainly gets you out of your comfort zone and allows you to navigate whirlwinds and undercurrents. Courage is the power to face forces stronger than you with determination and resolve. Being competitive is not about courage, but aiming to be number one and being capable of sustaining it equate to courage.

Within my own treasure chest, courage is something that I have developed in abundance. I only realized that in later years through my own self-reflection. It is an essential attribute of leadership and integral to any businessperson's life, because one has got to take risks, and courage helps to manage those highs and lows and make bold decisions. From my years at college to my work life and later as an entrepreneur, my courage helped me dive deep into risks that helped me learn how to transcend obstacles. In college, after three years of completing my science studies and at the end of the academic year, I chose to drop out of the course to start afresh in liberal arts. I left a successful career in banking to start a business with zero capital because I took a bet on my potential. I took that gamble as I firmly believed any other course of action would be detrimental to my interests. I took many more such risks in my life as a result of my relentless pursuit to transform lives and businesses, where courage was needed to break stereotypes.

All my decisions using courage did not always work in my favor. There were decisions such as the leveraged buyout of a company, which resulted in a significant loss for me. In hindsight, I ended up learning from this mistake, which eventually was applied in my success going forward.

Courage may be considered foolish if actions taken are not backed by rationale and prudence. However, I did go wrong and acted in haste, making mistakes, but I learned from this. I corrected the course of my hasty actions, and that made me worldly wise in my introspection. My conviction about *purpose* empowered my courage; as for me, it was always about the impact and never about greed or sinister motives. In this way, I was able to prevail over the hardships from my mistakes and still find a positive way forward.

When taking bold decisions, make sure they are backed with strong conviction and ensure you are ready to take the fallout as a positive learning opportunity.

Reflection Points

- Courage is what it takes to stand up against whirlwinds, which also requires strong conviction, coupled with the sincerity of purpose to take relentless actions.

- Courage comes from your faith and the purity of vision that acts as a beacon against confusion and uncertainties.

1.12. Relationships Empower Businesses to Build Lifelong Partnerships among Stakeholders

My values have always remained my guiding force in building my relationships. From my time at school with my teachers and school friends to my own family and my friends and business associates, my relationships have been my biggest collateral. These relationships gave me solace during times of crisis, great help in my difficult periods, and sound advice whenever I needed it.

In businesses too, my relationships with my stakeholders, especially with shareholders, greatly helped in my efforts to build the business. It is with the help of these relationships and their trust that I earned empowerment. I also worked tirelessly to develop a bond with my board members and C suite, where we all worked together to build an organization of substance and scale. I diligently engaged every stakeholder through a personalized relationship to ensure transparency and trust between them and me. I was careful to earn my respect through my deliverables and continued to build the relationship through my proven track record and commitment. Be it shareholders, banks, clients, or my employees, this remained my key result area. I would also like to touch upon the relationship I built with my colleagues, especially those who helped me build the organization. That relationship was not just work; I went beyond by building a relationship of trust and care where their holistic development, both professional and personally, remained my genuine concern. I was able to earn their respect by making sure they saw me as one of their family members.

However, the moot question was the salient feature in these relationships that cemented the bond. In my fundamental approach or strategy across most businesses, I chose substance where people's character matters and worked to ensure that people and corporate goals are fully aligned. I know well that the organizational value system and people's character will forge a great partnership. I was conscious that substance matters when I developed my wish list of target clients. They, too, prefer to deal with a business with people of character where high ethical values exist and where the company and its teams align with shared goals.

I have always dealt with the world's best clientele in my business history and proudly retained them as well. This was made possible because I built organizations where people were well aligned through a common bond of professional ethics. They provided ease of doing business and a seamless experience to their clients. I created organizations where relationships remained the cornerstone for all stakeholders, be it employees, clients, or others. Operational excellence cemented client relationships, ethical dealings, and governance.

In the thirty years of my business activities, my client relationships remained my most powerful support as I worked to create perpetual alliances that helped me expand the business. Those clients always came forward to endorse my proven track record and gave me a helping hand to develop business with them or others. In 2010 I started with one global bank, and by 2020 I had gained more than two hundred global multinationals in my portfolio with almost 95 percent retention. I grew with them and expanded through their support to others. The same is the case in context to my relationships with my C suite and with employees.

I was careful to foster a culture of "buddies" in the organization, where people trusted each other and would create situations through collaborative projects that would often test their relationships. I knew that proven and tested relationships foster bonds among colleagues and wanted to ensure that my colleagues were always able to rise above negativity and animosity to work in collaboration successfully. People were forbidden to speak in hushed tones behind anyone's back but instead encouraged to speak out when necessary, while bound by a shared vision.

My businesses were known for their impeccable reputation where a multitude of relationships and clients drove a tremendous value proposition from our dealings. Here is where colleagues saw trust and friendship blooming, shareholders found honest and sincere people to empower, and others saw a committed group of people bound by a relentless drive to uphold the integrity of relationships.

At EFS, or for that matter in most businesses and other dealings, there was always a common feeling of trust, transparency, and comfort due to my efforts in this regard.

Reflection Points

- At EFS we built a company culture where all embraced relationship needs as a primary element for our success.

- We worked hand in hand to create a lifelong bond with each other, including in the downstream organizations, while reaching out to all subordinate colleagues with the same zeal and spirit.

1.13. Leaders Must Use Self-Reflection to Excel

Self-reflection is yet another attribute that enables us to discover ourselves and calls for honest and deep introspection. One needs to review actions and their impact and outcomes. Self-reflection is a mirror to see through your rejections, evaluate your strengths and weaknesses, and consider changes you need to make to your character. This is something that helped me during my journey to discover myself, whether regarding my work-life goals, my family, or my extended relationships. The conclusions from my self-reflections helped me become a better human being and a more resilient person.

In the process of introspection of my wrongs, be it business failures or personal life, I learned a great deal. I was able to benefit my business from these insights greatly. For instance, at EFS, my current business, I used every bit of business prudence principles I learned in my past businesses. My zero tolerance for free cash flow and lean overhead was part of my self-reflection on my mistakes in previous ventures, not just from mistakes of the past, but I adapted lessons from my past successes too. I used my strategic mind and intrinsic cost knowledge to augment my business.

In my personal life, I also worked to build a stronger bond with my children by developing a relationship as a friend, rising above the conventional father-daughter relationship.

These self-reflections drove me to adopt the inclusive agenda of seeking a common good before self-good. These also contributed to the pursuit of status quos, be it inequality in the world or suffering. A good leader must take time to reflect in depth on the complexities of life and how everyone in the organization is affected. They should be able to balance a spiritually conscious and logical approach to those inequalities and wrongs.

Unless this reflection is done through deep introspection, communication with your audience will not be able to touch their hearts and minds in the way it must.

Reflection Points

- The output of reflection is self-awareness, self-consciousness, self-assessment, and a deep sense of your destiny, resulting in a harmonious relationship of the self with nature.

- This passionate energy has helped me to evolve immensely, and self-discovery enabled me to communicate with people much more effectively.

1.14. My Litmus Test to Rise as a Leader

Having been through very tough challenges in life, I, like everyone, found the arrival of COVID-19 to be indeed an event to remember. Despite its restrictions, with serious illness, death, travel chaos, and health panic all around, I was still traveling extensively till the end of February 2020. Unfortunately, to my dismay, the lockdown brought my life (which I felt fortunate to have) to a halt. I knew that none of that could take me down, but being at the helm to lead the company, I slowed down to assess what was coming.

On a personal level, I was unsettled with a life being led mostly within four walls. I was lucky that, due to the nature of my business, I was allowed to travel, so even the lockdown did not stop me. Though careful but never with a moment of fear in my heart, I took precautions but did mentally prepare myself for the eventuality of receiving a positive diagnosis. On a personal front, nothing deterred me from attending to my priorities, one of which was the home construction project that I started in April 2020! I continued going to the office and to my outdoor activities. However, it did require our family to employ all possible safeguards. Something that bothered me greatly was my younger daughter being in New York for school and away from the family.

However, with regard to work, there was an anxiety and unease watching as crises were unfolding. I was mindful that these events would possibly herald an end or at least a slowdown of our long stint of a business upturn—even fears of a severe downturn due to worldwide lockdowns and business losses.

We did, though, build sufficient checks and balances to maintain sustainability. In our efforts to guard against the unforeseen, we had some inherent measures already in place. However, there was no room for complacency, and we acted. The first measure was to protect our employees, as most of our men and women were frontline workers.

These were the true unsung heroes fighting the pandemic, while most of us were cuddled together with families in the safe silos of our houses. We ensured their workplace safety as well as assured our clients that we would be able to provide uninterrupted services. These measures helped to retain the confidence of employees and clients, both of which are essential business resilience needs. We went the extra mile to forge tactical retreats with those clients to reduce costs as downturns impacted them. In this journey of resilience, cost management was critical. We had a double whammy with clients reducing footprint and seeking discounts and cost overruns due to employee safety protocols and supply chain disruption in materials cost. We took a deep dive into cost efficiencies; we could find many avenues from rent, bank interest, and supplier bargains with zero job losses. Realizing the significant reduction in revenues and margins, we moved to build new service lines. While the COVID-19 crisis was unleashing its wrath, it was also opening doors for more unique opportunities to pursue.

We have always had our eyes on that aspect: to seek opportunity in crises. We started with the disinfection business, and, with the fear of COVID-19 always present, this led to a new business to address the requirements for disinfection to be performed at the highest level.

In just three months, at the end of the June quarter, while we lost 30 percent in revenues and over 25 percent in profits, we were able to bring in additional profits with new service lines and reduce expenses by 15 percent. In essence, during this difficult time, we delivered our historically best quarter, with a net increase of 24 percent in net profits.

We did it because we had our people on our side. Be it frontline workers, managers, or management, all took this challenge as a part of their collective resolve. We did not relent and went on to take newer measures, and we gave our shareholders their best year, with an over 25 percent increase in profits and the best-ever balance sheet that the company was able to achieve.

We not only closed the year with great numbers but gave bonuses, protected jobs, and even gave increments. We did not leave off there but arranged to immunize 75 percent of our staff and gave clients an overall 15 percent discount in the form of savings. These were some of the many measures we took to mitigate the harsh reality of the COVID-19 virus.

We had our share of worries and remorse, with only two individuals who sadly lost their lives among the strong workforce of eighteen thousand. However, the learnings in resilience led us to focus even more on excellence and business continuity. The COVID-19 pandemic, with its dark realities, also taught some great lessons on resilience. While the world has touched upon the social side of resilience in terms of family, relationships, and behaviors, at EFS the pandemic taught me about the power of discipline, positivity, well-being, teamwork, and transformation. In this pandemic fight, transformation transcended from an option to become a necessity; whether it was telephony, remote working, or service innovation, I saw transformation at EFS at its best.

The COVID-19 pandemic gave us opportunities in abundance to transform, and our technology preparedness was one such opportunity.

Despite market downturn and being 10 percent over the budget, EFS was able to retain 100 percent of its employees with zero deductions and also create more job opportunities and offer sustainable service delivery, as well as develop technology integration along with proactive client and staff engagement. The business has additionally broadened its scope with the introduction of Bio Clean services under FM solutions, which include disinfection, deep cleaning, indoor air quality, water tank cleaning, and more.

The preparedness and response by EFS to COVID-19 focuses on health and safety for all employees, clients, and the community, adhering to local and international regulations and business continuity. EFS has also been very proactive in supporting endeavors and initiatives by the UAE leadership, the use of technology and innovation through remote working, automation, decontamination, real-time monitoring, and financial safety and security. EFS strides also include initiatives done for employee engagement, communication, learning, and development and continued client and staff engagement as well as satisfaction.

Reflection Point

- COVID-19 pandemic learnings have once again reminded us that being resilient is the only significant advantage to ride through the waves of turbulence. EFS is not only built on resilience but has transformed to remain relevant and ahead of the curve with our COVID-19 maneuvers.

2. THE PEOPLE-FIRST APPROACH

The concept of "people first" evolved with my journey at EFS, where business was centered around people. These employees directly render more than two-thirds of its services, and most of the cost of running the company is also related to them. I realized the need for employee happiness as integral to company well-being. I adopted "people first" as my crucial strategy to build an organization where employee happiness and self-actualization actually mattered.

The concept of the people-first approach is not a new one, but the successful application of the same requires a significant effort to embed in the culture of the business. The approach needs to become a daily way of life rather than a sign of tokenism by holding a few activities or initiatives. This is applicable to all business types, whether with a few handfuls of staff or a large ground force.

2.1. Blue-Collar Workers, the Real Unsung Heroes—Their Engagement and Inclusion

Being the CEO of a company with an eighteen-thousand-strong facilities management workforce, with two-thirds of it being a blue-collar workforce, my work to ensure the success of our employee engagement process has been intense and rewarding. But it is a complex task to manage the expectations of these employees and to gain their trust.

My interaction with the large section of blue-collar workers in my company gave me a new perspective and insights into the need to include all of them in the corporate mainstream.

At the beginning, I could see that the state of blue-collar workers had its issues and needed a fresh review. I was surprised to see that the blue-collar workers were never addressed by their real names but were called workers, laborers, blue-collar, or trades.

However, in reality, these people require respect like any other employee, each having their own worth and intrinsic value. What seemed to matter most were only their productivity parameters, basic needs, salaries, and facilities but not their holistic needs. I realized this fundamental disconnect had to change.

Their contribution to the company is fundamental to its own performance, as they are the main drivers of service efficiency, productivity, and quality. In reality, these are the real "unsung heroes" of most companies.

I determined that my engagement with these people would become a priority, and I went the extra mile to align these aspects in my people engagement policy.

Eventually, it became a driving purpose in my life to champion their cause. Why not? These were among the foremost champions in my company. Whether it had to do with their living standards, social woes, or financial worries, I roped in my entire organization to address this and work beyond the workplace "do's" to addressing their holistic needs. The writing on the wall was clear: blue-collar workforce engagements must focus on their development and progression, not just on the perks and facilities.

This segment of our workforce took center stage in our human resources strategy. But I have learned much from my own life experiences, which helped me to align my organizational priorities with the people who work for it. This provided me with a sneak preview of their issues and hardships. I must admit that issues revolving around the lives of blue-collar workers made a far-reaching impact on my perspectives of life. Indeed, what I learned about their hardships transformed my entire mindset, leading to a 360-degree change in my engagement with these people.

I realized that most organizations do little to elevate their employees to their full potential, with no concrete measures for

> The writing on the wall was clear: blue-collar workforce engagements must focus on their development and progression, not just on the perks and facilities.

their inclusion into the organizational mainstream. Usually, their relationship with employees is primarily transactional, confined to conventional employee well-being and work-related aspects. In general, there is a vast lacuna in this particular type of employee engagement, with limited employer outreach. This requires a major fix.

Especially in labor-centric industries such as manufacturing, services, logistics, and construction, with more than 50 percent representation for blue-collar workers, not much is factored into any ways to address their holistic needs beyond a basic fundamental well-being.

Their development is vital to the overall welfare of the company, and yet this is often overlooked. Even employee well-being is mainly done based on conventional staff-centric measures, achieving limited motivational impact and not a 360-degree engagement.

Not only businesses but also governments need to contemplate developing action plans to elevate their standards, as these employees represent almost 50 percent of the global workforce.

An initiative for blue-collar workforce development primarily requires strong management support to achieve its desired impact. For seamless integration of these workers into the mainstream organization, the stakeholders have to make conscious efforts to tweak company culture.

It is a no-brainer that a higher level of progression for the blue-collar workforce is a definitive business booster, as it improves employee morale and brings substantial financial benefits to the company as well as to the employee. However, it is a complex task and requires the strong execution of a learning and development strategy, primarily focusing on reskilling/upskilling.

Success stories of some of the most exceptional organizations, including Unilever, P&G, and Ford, show the success of such strategies.

A successful progression plan very specific to blue-collar employees is the fundamental need to uplift them and help address the tough challenges they face. Positive executive engagement is required to make it work, and just compassionate postures will do nothing. This progression of blue-collar employees will serve as a genuinely sustainable business advantage.

Over the last ten years during my close encounters with the workers, talking with them about their prevailing issues has helped me understand the power of compassion and how steps, as mentioned earlier, transform their lives. These blue-collar workers have been the *real* heroes, the boots on the ground, who made all the difference to the success of EFS. Their contribution is the most significant differentiator of our success story, and to pay them their dues, we continue to seek their input and participation as well as work tirelessly to improve their motivation levels.

Due to the humble beginning that we have put into motion, we succeeded by achieving over 85 percent employee retention. Thanks to those valuable employees, we have retained more than 97 percent of our clients and achieved 20 percent compound annual growth rate for the last decade.

In my outreach to build a true people-first organization, I realized that the company's human resources issues rest with the engagement of its blue-collar workforce. Their inclusivity in the organizational mainstream mattered, so I worked to build a unique bond by focusing on their core issues. I created a dedicated strategy based on six pillars of worker welfare: mental health and well-being, family, quality living, recreation, financial safety, and learning and development.

These elements were made integral in the operating plan and execution. To ensure its desired outcomes, I directly linked this to management's key result areas to provide the required results. I led this engagement along with my C-suite colleagues.

Organizations need to build a culture with motivated executives and managers to achieve an ideal engagement with this section of the workforce. Building trust with them requires understanding their needs and behaviors, which are deeply rooted in their ecosystem. *We have to build a bridge that connects their minds and hearts to reach them.*

Reflection Point

- To correct this long-term anomaly, it is time for company stakeholders to first understand the general mindsets of the blue-collar workers and their world outlook. These people have difficulties to confront, as well as a trust deficit with the social system itself. Some have deeply embedded grievances derived from lifelong hardships. Business leaders have to make conscious efforts to push for reforming their organizations to address these issues.

2.2. In Pursuit of Building a Value-Based Organization through Team Chemistry

I was well aware that a people-first organization could not be built in a day, so we started working on many fronts such as values embodiment at the enterprise level, developing a shared vision with inclusivity, diversity, and passion-driven ownership at its foundation.

To build a sustainable enterprise, businesses must look beyond performance, annual budgets, financial performance, and bonus or dividend payouts and instead must look at all stakeholders' perspectives as well.

In any organization this matters greatly, but more specifically, in my context of being in a service industry, the people perspective and values embodiment were critical.

Just as with the many companies and professional jobs of my career, there were lessons to learn. However, my evolving journey at EFS was very fulfilling. The role at EFS transformed me, helped to leverage my strengths, and provided opportunities to fill in gaps to overcome my weaknesses with a holistic impact. Although there are multiple factors behind this success, the one dominant force was my learning from past failures and the deep introspections I was led to. As mentioned earlier, one of the salient aspects of my journey at EFS was adopting the people-first approach.

In my perpetual quest for creating impact in my life and my professional work, whether a task, job, or mission, team selection and its specific dynamics of people, systems, and structure were the fundamental ethos of my journey at EFS.

> I realized that a good team effort and apt chemistry between the players is needed to build the conviction to deliver results.

Team means people, and my basis for selecting a team and the people therein is always based on a *values* embodiment and other specific and vital attributes of discipline, attitude, and commitment.

In most of my dealings with people, and in my professional reviews of people's strengths and weaknesses, I have emphasized that people attributes include personal, professional, and functional aspects, and we put together a comprehensive plan to assess these attributes and embody them.

I realized that a good team effort and apt chemistry between the players is needed to build the conviction to deliver results. This will ensure that the team understands that these accomplishments will have a definitive holistic impact resulting in their own higher self-actualization. With an eye on a shared vision, I ensured that they saw these engagements and accomplishments as opportunities for their own professional and self-development. I prioritized forging alliances in most of my work, be it with colleagues or with companies, based on genuine partnerships with shared goals and values throughout all of my life.

I cobbled these alliances together based on deep mutual respect and relationships to build people's convictions, be it employees, clients, suppliers, or shareholders. These remained as vital prerequisites to most of my business or personal dealings. I would go out of my way to focus on this prerequisite whenever building new teams or putting up a new project.

I also ensured that the team had shared values and ownership in every mission by conviction, and in alignment with their self-development goals from the desired specific outcomes. I wanted them to see the benefits of the learnings from the journey as life enriching. I am proud of the relationships that I have built with my colleagues. They were made aware that these learnings are integral to their interests. I made sure that my colleagues were mindful of the understandings, not just the success but the failures too, with deep introspections that would enable them to be more resilient.

Reflection Point

- In most team engagements, I make it a point to engage the team to first buy into my leadership through the virtue of respect, as well as respect for their own tangible contribution for the purpose at hand.

2.3. Work-Life Goal Analytics

Work life span, by far, is the longest phase of our life cycle and its three phases, which include early life, work life, and retirement. Work life also remains the biggest influencer of our overall life. The initial or early part of our life prepares us for our work life, as this is the longest and most engaging period in context to its complex ecosystem. The last of these is retirement. It is often considered a fearful prospect due to fear of the unknown, its change management implications, and other lifestyle woes. These also compound people's worries and often give them a sense of guilt, as they believe that their retirement period could have been better had they been able to manage their work-life balance and duly factored the needs of retirement while in the professional phase. In an average work life, due to the other priorities that must be faced, fewer and fewer can claim to do this balancing act with success.

It is therefore necessary to adopt personal, financial, and work-life goal setting as an essential approach to our lifelong planning. This serves as a guiding force to evaluate our milestones as we adjust or recalibrate them across the cycles of our life and its changing needs. However, do we all, in reality, plan or know how to envision what weight we have to provide to each of these goals? Of course, we do keep changing these weights and their settings according to the individual situation at a given stage of our life. This is the moot point: Do we know how to measure them and make our decision based on their given weights? We must know that any critical life-changing decision must take into account the particular weight that we have provided for that goal.

For instance, if in the early stage we most prioritize our professional goals, then, in that case, the weight will indeed be much higher than the personal or financial goals. Therefore, a new job offer must be analyzed on that basis, not just because it has a very high financial element to it and vice versa. It is indeed a stark reality that we all know about the importance of work-life dynamics but often do not objectively allocate sufficient time to delve into details to manage this. We are often confronted with confused mindsets about how to reach crucial work-life-related decisions. I therefore recommend that people must use analytics to provide weight to each of their goals.

However, before we delve into analytics, we need to assess the various components that comprise our work and personal life goals. When it comes to work or professional goals and their components, such as job context, prospects, and overall job satisfaction, there is the need for a sufficient bare-minimum weight given within a range that may change at different stages of life, such as in our thirties, forties, and fifties. However, this must not be less than a certain minimum of the overall weight, since work always remains the focal point of our lifetime. It is important that this should be fully aligned to almost a similar weight on bare-minimum financial needs. One has to take a sane view of his or her personal life goals, such as work-life balance, family, health, and self-actualization.

Do we all ever diligently look at these or, for that matter, know about their aspects and what influences them? These are classified between personal, financial, and work as professional, financial, self-actualization, family, and health. As elaborated above, these weights do vary at an individual level, as each has his or her preference/requisites, as well as the fact that these often do change at different stages of life. However, these personal goals must be integrated with work life to build a good work-life balance. This is something that the workforce is actively seeking, especially the millennials.

It is not always possible to have a standard model and achieve a perfect mix between professional goals and the personal level, but it is indeed essential that we build or strike the right balance *between professional and personal goals.* These have to be managed and continuously recalibrated. Another critical aspect to be considered is how to build the right chord between reality and a wish list. There are different stages of our life—the early stage of our thirties and forties, the fifties and sixties, and old age—and these have events therein such as family issues (marriage, kids, and their education), health, hobbies, etc. However, in context to any of these goals, which have a vital importance to personal life, individual preferences may have different weights due to a particular situation. But even so, they need to have a bare-minimum criteria assigned, as each of these are essential for balanced and holistic life goals. While you could have a significant allocation of weightage for family, it still needs to balance with other components such as health and self. These weights also need to be aligned with professional life goals, what we call work-life balance.

Reflection Point

- In work life, professional and financial goals have to be well integrated to be properly balanced with due weight for each.

2.4. A Business Case Made for Happiness at the Workplace

A *paradigm shift* is taking place in employee happiness and wellness. Rather than simply involving monetary rewards, recent polls have shown that employees in the UAE care more about career advancement and job satisfaction. Millennials and Gen Z, today's youth, are increasing their share in the workforce and disrupting conventional corporate culture to place more importance on individual well-being and happiness. In today's business environment, happiness is essential for enhancing productivity and innovation at the workplace and building a progressive nation.

I believe that it is time for the private and public sectors to step forward and focus on happiness as a key driver in business sustainability and growth for three essential reasons.

Firstly, real-life examples and studies indicate that happiness boosts employee productivity, largely affecting a company's bottom line. A study by the University of Warwick determined that employee happiness increased productivity by 12 percent. Focusing on workforce wellness also reduces absenteeism; happy employees take ten times less sick days than unhappy employees. These results directly impact the profitability of firms. The firms featured in Fortune's 100 Best Companies to Work For enjoyed a 7 percent higher stock price valuation compared to the rest of the market from 1998 to 2005.

The world's best-regarded employer, Google, is the perfect example of believing that monetary incentives are insufficient to keep their workers engaged. Google has several leaders whose sole responsibility is to keep employees happy and productive, because Google truly believes that it is the people who make them what they are today.

Secondly, the economies that have succeeded the most are those in which the private sector and the government have worked in tandem and have shared the same core values.

Lastly, as the country's workforce brings in more youth, it is necessary to understand and cater to their needs to retain top talent and drive future economic growth. In recent studies, both globally and regionally, the millennial and Gen Z generations value creativity, autonomy, and transparency in the workplace over just financial compensation. Today's workforce places development opportunities above all else. If we want to retain the best talent from the younger generation, valuing their happiness is the critical factor in accomplishing that.

Despite the evidence, for many organizations the idea of employee happiness can seem too abstract to be acted upon, so it does not always receive the prioritization it deserves. Employees are often the most significant assets of an organization, but it is equally important that organizations treat employees like people and not assets. The starting point is to attract and retain the best, give them support and encouragement, and make them feel that they are necessary to the organization's central goal.

Furthermore, *increasing employee engagement can open the door for business leaders to improve their profitability* by putting resources into employee welfare and work environment satisfaction, thereby setting themselves apart from the competition in many ways as they achieve business goals. Improving employee happiness can also be achieved through simple ways, by promoting a culture that encourages coworkers to help each other out, meditation, engaging in sports or fitness activities together, corporate social responsibility (CSR) activities, and reflecting on a few things to be grateful for at work, among others.

Reflection Points

- In conclusion, if we implement happiness and wellness initiatives into our corporate culture, our businesses' productivity and job satisfaction will see a significant increase and directly impact the economy's growth and corporate profitability. This will undoubtedly contribute toward building a more modern and progressive nation.

- Money remains a prominent driver in the happiness of employees, be it salary, annual increments, or bonuses; employees respond to this more positively. For instance, adjusting living index parity in annual wage reviews is a must for companies to build employees' trust and promote fairness.

2.5. An Adjustment of Living Index Parity in Annual Wage Reviews Is a Must for Companies to Build Employee Trust and Promote Fairness

Employees' expectations for a salary raise in line with any spike in the cost-of-living index is fair and must not be ignored. And when it's not done, this is cited as a usual employee grievance.

A cost-of-living raise is an increase in pay to ensure the employee's salary is the same during a period of inflation, if any. This demand must not be lost in translation, citing market conditions or a comparative salary index to tone down this request. Without a cost-of-living lift, workers are left with less real money.

Cost-of-living raises are also known as cost-of-living adjustments

(COLAs). We also refer to this as the consumer price index, which is an approximation of how much someone must spend to attain a certain level of well-being. It measures the price of a basket of goods and services that an average household can buy.

Companies should see this as a genuine need to recognize best practices. In fact, following these practices sets the requisite standards for effective employee engagement and ensures workforce happiness.

Increments arising from work-related improvements and promotion-related assessments must not form a part of this review. Still, any consideration on a rise in living-index-related adjustments should be a separate exercise. Individual employee performance, divisional profits, company performance, and living cost adjustments should be the *four main criteria* for the annual compensation evaluation reviews.

Indeed, each can have its weightage, but wage increment must be a critical factor in living index parity in an appraisal review. Companies must consider this element as a cost and factor it into budgetary estimates.

I realize that any such move may be tough in current market conditions. Still, all organizations should be aware that it is fundamental to their well-being for employees to be able to meet their basic living needs and is indeed tied to a company's overall performance.

It is imperative for finance departments in organizations to factor in this need, and they must provide this as an essential cost differential in their forecasts.

The living index cost primarily covers their holistic needs, such as food, utilities, rent, recreation, entertainment, communications, clothing, transportation, healthcare, and education.

From these costs, rent and education are the two significant variants that must be a part of any wage review. No doubt, in recent years, rent differentials in the UAE have been a matter of greater—or lesser—concern. This index has tilted both southward and northward, and it is fair that we engage employees, either way, to communicate about the impact on both the company and the employee. It is a tough call, as markets continue to remain hostile to any cost escalations.

However, suppose we observe fairness as a company's *value*. In that case, there is no option but to waive this consideration, however difficult it may be, because such a measure can be a booster for employee morale.

Reflection Point

- There can be many ways to arrive at a fair conclusion based on merit. However, regarding the living index, there cannot be any debate, as it is based on publicly available data. To ease the pressure on themselves, companies must factor this into their contractual engagements and when preparing their forecasts. This must be implemented across the entire workforce and not only on selective criteria.

2.6. Building the Business Case for Progression

As an old proverb wisely states, there is an opportunity in every crisis. In times of austerity, innovation is the only way out. In moments of introspection and strategy reviews driven by market pressures, management delves into their various departments' working reality, devising ways and means for business robustness and agility. In a push for this strategic renaissance, primarily when driven by recessionary challenges, the role of human resources, a key business enabler, comes under close focus.

Learning and development are differentiators within multiple functions that can be greatly leveraged to get great results. Although not many see this cost optimizer as more than a way to ensure service excellence and an employee motivation tool, HR is a powerful resource for employee progression, emerging as an important enabler in organizational transformation. We have learned many lessons in times of business turbulence, but this one is the most critical: don't just look for out-of-box solutions when the going gets difficult but instead look *within* the box to seek the opportunities that lie within. Employee progression is one such opportunity, often driven by innovation that we have come across when seeking solutions for cost efficiencies.

Employee progression is also a key element of succession planning, where younger employees are developed as future replacements for aging senior staff. Succession serves the need for knowledge retention in the company and can be an alternative to the costly and challenging task of hiring from outside the company for key roles.

Don't just look for out-of-box solutions when the going gets difficult but instead look *within* the box to seek the opportunities that lie within.

While most business leaders understand the benefits of progression, only a few organizations accord the needed attention to ensuring it.

Progression helps to build service excellence and staff motivation and brings the organization financial benefits. This is becoming an active tool to achieve staff cost efficiencies—and, besides, its other advantages are startling! How does this work?

It creates an environment of learning and development that prompts people to work to move up in the organization, resulting in financial restitution and a feeling of recognition, plus rewards that spike higher motivation levels.

Our organization has accomplished nearly a 10 percent progression over a workforce of twelve thousand in the past seven years, which is an impressive milestone.

How does the enterprise derive cost savings from this strategic push? When an employee in progression moves up in the organization and replaces senior employees, they bring cost savings due to salary differentials. Stepping up to the next level increases salary, position, and perks and replaces the higher-grade bracket with a lower-grade bracket that means savings for companies. In essence, progressions undoubtedly result in definite cost savings, in some cases as high as 20 percent in compensations.

However, the complex part of this contract condition in our workforce-centric organization is how to accomplish this, where 70 percent of the cost is salaries, and the glide path of savings over the life cycle of the contract is indeed herculean. The salaries revision is an annual feature, and achieving savings is difficult as a headcount purge is not always possible. However, adopting the progression approach has emerged as a powerful and effective tool.

Empowered by strong learning and development, this model has helped organizations as well as EFS, and I can confirm that, across most of our contracts, we have achieved this by successfully employing this measure. This move has 360-degree benefits—sought by employees, loved by HR managers, and actively bought into by our clients.

Apart from other conventional employee motivation tools, progression is becoming the most powerful employee retention and brand positioning enabler.

Reflection Point

- Employee progression has become relevant in our FM industry as clients seek to move to a new generation of contracts where the glide path of savings is integral to the contract performance.

2.7. There Is Work to Be Done Integrating Millennials

Do we know who those millennials are? Are they just defined by the fact they became adults in the twenty-first century? Or is there much more about them that we need to understand? Sure, they tend to be well informed, be independent, and have much more clarity of life, which I am sure only a few of the earlier generations had. They are not fearful, speak for themselves, and are often assured and self-possessed.

More millennials are joining the workforce, and their presence requires a 360-degree shift in the workplace perspective. These young men and women bring with them many challenges and opportunities indeed. We need to apply logic and rationale in dealing with them. Their transition into any work environment can become a mammoth challenge if we don't engage them while at the same time we are sensitive to their needs.

Ignoring their strengths and aspirations and not being able to connect with their specific needs are often issues. In most workplaces, employee engagement is left to the human resources department, and this creates a limited mentoring bandwidth. Management needs to take significant steps to integrate this workforce for any successful transition.

A holistic organization policy is thus necessary with inclusion for all stakeholders. Due to their endless appetite for quest and change, the workplace ecosystem needs to be tweaked specifically to suit millennials. Stakeholders must make conscious efforts to create such opportunities and take the requisite measures to align them with the larger organizational goals.

Realistically, one has to analyze the workplace culture and its preparedness at the organization level to integrate this workforce. This requires the senior employees to shed their inhibitions and adopt a role model approach instead of asking the newer lot to change. Or, worse, try to use the usual old-fashioned parenting or motivational tools.

The fact is that conventional approaches will not work. Avoid drawing conclusions about the need to show more responsibility or respect. Apply logic to each of their actions before evaluating their merits or lack of same. It is essential that the senior employees recalibrate their outlook.

When millennials interact in à la mode workplaces, their professional interfaces with nonmillennials sometimes are impacted by too many inhibitions on either side. When they seek clarity on work-life balance, they can sometimes be disparaged for asking questions.

Millennials, for their part, sometimes complain that their credentials are not often reviewed on merits when they scale the corporate ladder. And instead, unambiguous conclusions are drawn, undermining their merits.

They are the generation with a marked difference, and the abundance of information has made them worldly wise, eloquent, and tolerant of difference. Having been raised under the philosophy, "follow your dreams," this confidence can spill over into the realms of entitlement and narcissism.

Their expectations of equality are not based on age but rather on the simple definition of merits. Millennials don't like taking "orders" and expect a professional decorum.

Reflection Points

- The ambitions of this new wave of employees must not be seen as misplaced optimism or unrealistic expectations.

- It is important to maintain a high level of respectful interaction that does not lead to disillusionment or the lowering of standards presently in place.

2.8. Motivating a Diverse Workforce

During my corporate journey, including ten years at the helm of EFS, I have realized that promises or actions cannot deliver results without a strong leader who can make an impact.

I began to explore ways to ensure that my actions and those of my team create transformational results that can make a real difference to the company and, ultimately, to its people. This included making sure that the benefits derived from that impact are not just accrued to a select few but to all employees and their families.

This is no easy task at EFS; with a staff of over eighteen thousand and their families spanning across more than twenty-one countries and three subcontinents to think about, we realized the power and potential of an elevated workforce at the very earliest stages. We knew that the company's employees were the formidable force behind its success, its track record, and its growth—and not just the management and executives but more than fifteen thousand general staff comprised of the blue-collar workforce.

> Promises or actions cannot deliver results without a strong leader who can make an impact.

We remain focused and vigilant to ensure that these people remain part of the *mainstream corporate strategy*—I have no interest in tokenism and shallow gestures. We therefore set about creating an inclusive and coherent culture within the organization whereby everyone understands the role and importance of on-the-ground workforce engagement. Our objective was to make them feel elated and engaged. However, connecting with such a sizeable workforce and bringing them into mainstream organizational engagement was tricky, complicated, and daunting. Employee engagement on this scale needed an innovative touch. Another challenge we faced was the series of market downturns that constrained our capital to support this initiative. How could we maintain a balance between the due credits and perks needed for our people versus the limitations of our resources?

First, we established what it was that we wanted to achieve. Many blue-collar workers who come to this region worldwide have very low self-actualization levels. To gain their confidence, leaders needed to devise strategies that were focused on elevating their holistic needs. Building employee trust and instilling faith in the organization was our main task. As a leadership team, we mapped their needs and their perspectives and sought to understand the key issues that were focal to their interests.

Most people and organizations often get lost in salary and compensation issues when looking at the motivational needs of their core workforce. They seldom look at other critical drivers of worker engagement. For example, you might pay well, but all other efforts are in vain if you don't pay people on time.

It is often specific sensitivities that matter. The personal living conditions and the day-to-day upkeep of employees need to be appropriately comfortable, along with the provision of good facilities and amenities. For instance, telephone and Wi-Fi, family demands, and finance management are essential factors. These drive worker engagement to higher levels.

There also needs to be an internal communication strategy for staff to interact with their site leadership and apply for training and development opportunities. This plays a critical role in bridging the gap to gain trust.

So it is not just sweat, words, and actions that matter—these must transform into *real impact*. And impact means considering the social and economic ecosystem of the workforce. Their family-centric needs must be built into the company's employee engagement strategy as well.

At EFS, we have extended our CSR initiatives to the extended families of our workforce by introducing child education programs, health insurance for aging parents, and support for communities during national crises. These are just some of the key measures that we have adopted, strengthening our bond with our entire workforce.

However, salary is primarily a market-driven factor that few can mitigate. As long as your structure is aligned to the markets and you can manage your costs, you must concentrate on the other key elements that set the dominant faith and relationship with your staff.

Reflection Point

- Companies must not use corporate social responsibility as a checklist to tick off; instead, they must seek to build a culture that encompasses its real impact on all stakeholders.

2.9. Building a Compassionate Organization

The concept of a compassionate organization emanates from the organizational culture and respect for its values, where everyone embraces these as a matter of ownership and not simply as part of a job.

At EFS, we knew that the company had to go the extra mile to bring a compassionate touch to its organizational mainstream as an employer of a large blue-collar workforce. We wanted to factor in the due compassion needed for the blue-collar workers in context with their inherent social-economic backgrounds. We wanted to ensure that our organization has factored in this sensitivity and has recognized its needs. These workers need to be dealt with in a sensitive manner, and to motivate them, a trust-building campaign will need multiple compassionate initiatives. Therefore, we embarked on a mission to overhaul our staff welfare and the human resources department. But there is a much more emphatic outreach across all faculties to recognize the cause of compassion, especially when blue-collar workers represent two-thirds of our workforce. We were careful to enforce this mandate across all facets of the organization, be it communication, events, facilities, or learning and development. For instance, as mentioned earlier, all leadership tiers, from supervisors to managers, were to visit residential staff quarters on a fortnightly basis. This was an attempt to instill workers' trust by creating a bond and helping these managers understand the elements of compassion that needed their attention. The idea of them spending time with their blue-collar colleagues was also to understand their issues beyond just company engagement.

2.10. CSR as a People-Centric Measure, Not Just a Corporate Dashboard Credential

Value-based organizations have to take cognizance of all stakeholders. The moot question is, Who are these? In reality, we don't consider anyone to be a stakeholder other than employees, shareholders, clients, and suppliers. However, there is another perspective to look beyond. At EFS, I included family, community, nation, and environment as our stakeholders. In the context involving each of these stakeholders, we assume responsibility. We, therefore, built an exhaustive initiative to support these objectives.

In this regard, family elements were made integral to company HR policies and initiatives where each aspect was well factored. The environment aspect was covered through health, safety, environment, and quality organization frameworks that outlined elaborate steps, and national interests were embedded in compliance and community programs.

However, in context to the community, we built comprehensive measures to highlight and address the cause of the enterprise's social responsibility. This was also a way to help employees understand the cause of social responsibility to promote coherence, compassion, and community support. We wanted the organization to embed CSR as a culture, not just as a feature on the corporate credential dashboard.

Being an organization with many workers living in communities that require help led to great success. We were quickly able to make an impact with various initiatives. This push also acted as a catalyst in our intent to build a compassionate organization with inclusivity. We first started education aid for the workers' children who showed an exemplary attitude toward pursuing studies. Still, it was important to maintain inclusivity in terms of region, financial background, and other merits. The idea of CSR was always linked to those community interests that a large EFS workforce would connect with. From rehabilitation of flood-affected communities in India to earthquakes in Nepal, the Syrian refugees, the blast that occurred in Lebanon, and the wildfires that devastated Australia, EFS was among the first responders.

While we responded to natural communities, we also worked closely with government and private bodies to support many neighborhood programs in many countries to provide better hygiene, develop sustainable waste initiatives, and energy to recycling. We also began initiatives to help support community interests to provide programs for mental health, financial planning, and upskilling workshops.

The concept of CSR at EFS was to rise beyond just being seen cleaning beaches or running blood donation camps. In 2019, EFS created a department named EHSAAS, which means realization. The goal was to bring social responsibility into mainstream organizational activities and further its impact. CSR at EFS was self-owned by people and never pushed on, but more than one hundred staff immediately joined the program when it was first launched, and now it has over five hundred volunteers making a difference. It is not about earning brownie points but instead a way for people to increase their own self-actualization. I feel it is an essential requirement to build a great enterprise. An effective CSR program not only helps in brand elevation but also helps to bring more significant connections with employees.

Social responsibility, in essence, emanates from our values. How does it matter, and why do individuals have to adopt it? Some assume it is not their work to do. Many people think that all social responsibility causes are only the responsibility of governments and institutions.

However, in reality, human beings are dependent on each other, and with issues of community interests or civil society, where social causes need attention, all must come forward. This becomes a matter of social responsibility for everyone to take action. Whether it concerns the environment, public safety, health, or just compassion itself, it requires an individual conviction from everyone to create change.

Therefore, I strongly advocate that we need social responsibility to be viewed by all as a part of collective participation. It should be an essential motivator linked to everyone's self-actualization goals, and we must do everything to pursue this impact.

Companies, big or small, need to take gigantic steps to build an organization where everyone owns social responsibility as an inspiring exercise in self-motivation and a shared goal with all stakeholders. Furthermore, companies need to develop a culture where these become perpetual initiatives, not simply acts of tokenism.

For instance, we wanted to uphold diversity and inclusion with an eye on fairness and employee well-being. It was an attempt to boost compassion based on the fact that we have an over 2:3 ratio of employees operating as our blue-collar workforce. To accomplish this, we embarked on multiple projects that were designed to be an integral component of executives' and managers' employee engagement programs. All executives were required to visit and access staff accommodations, and C-suite executives also were required to visit workers' accommodations. Through its EHSAAS initiative, the company would organize monthly campaigns that included mental health, reducing carbon footprints, and also addressing community compassion-related aspects such as people of determination, people in financial distress, and refugees, including relief operations, and other works that were desperately needed during national calamities that occurred worldwide. It was developed to be a shared vision for all, not simply a company- or CEO-driven campaign.

Over the many years of my business life, I have seen campaigns and significant pledges by large companies to these efforts. Whether these commitments were made as part of their conviction to support compassionate operations or as a watershed to appease global concerns for international communities, they still did a great amount of good for many social causes.

In my role as CEO, I have always emphasized that this needs our team's conviction, and that our company's CSR must demonstrate compassion and determination to make a difference. All campaigns that we undertook were based on a careful survey of impact assessment, as being a small company we have limited resources and must assure that the resources we deploy and allocate deliver results where needed.

We were careful to use only the appropriate terminologies to remove biases in the organization. In all our dealings with the blue-collar workforce, whether directly or indirectly, we were careful to use only words that showed respect for the workers and their functions. The organization was required from the top down to ensure that engagement with blue-collar workers was not just a routine HR engagement but rather a holistic well-being exercise where all aspects of compassion were considered. It was not centered overtly on individuals but as a general cause to promote the purpose of compassion.

At EFS, it initially started as an employee engagement exercise. Eventually it became a culture that caught the outside world's attention with clients, competition, and media recognizing this strong push. EFSians started to identify with this particular element by calling themselves "Proud to Be EFSians." Later on, with years of robust engagements in delving into the workers' most grueling issues, EFS had developed a culture where blue-collar well-being mattered greatly, and the organization has placed its policies and infrastructure to support this well-being in the best possible way.

The six pillars of worker welfare purely drive EFS. They include safety and security, well-being, quality living, self and family, community participation, and workplace happiness. These were devised to promote holistic well-being. EFS brought in a concept of multiple initiatives to improve the interface with employees. These activities included offering a quarterly breakfast with the CEO and workers' day, where the management swaps roles with housekeeping and technical staff, helping them carry out their chores as a token of their gratitude toward them, as well as organizing an annual carnival where the entire organization comes forward to host blue-collar workers with a day filled with fun and fervor.

Now after eight years in a row, the EFS carnival has become one of the most significant and most powerful forces to reckon with in motivating its employees, reminding others why employee engagement matters and why this is even more so the case for blue-collar engagement. The carnival is a platform for elevating self-actualization by applauding unique talent and artists and praising the sportsmanship spirit. It also honors the blue-collar staff and their families, with the Compassionate Awards recognizing members from all walks of life, be it needy and deserving, aged parents or children's education, special needs, or family reunions for young mothers away from home.

Over the years, several encounters like these have helped to intensify a profound understanding for this segment of employees and the larger blue-collar society with *compassion*. EFS has over 15 percent progression in the blue-collar workforce, with more than a hundred staff rising through progression in the corporate ladder, reaching even up to three to four promotions in just thirty-six months.

By way of example, an office assistant, Arati, now working in the corporate office, has risen from a housekeeper to earning five times her original salary and rising through three promotions in just thirty-six months. Like her, there are many such cases. And this drive of compassion and recognizing excellence was based on a developmental perspective with an eye on the overall self-actualization. Many acts of compassion, CSR campaigns, or various awards were introduced to bolster this cause.

Reflection Points

- CSR is not about the quantum of money and time you spend but has more to do with engaging your employees with sincerity and inspiring their own potential to do good in the greater society that surrounds them.

- We strategically isolated empathy from compassion to build a more sustainable environment with developmental and correctional aspects.

- Our engagement with blue-collar workers was targeted at their holistic development, where their economic upliftment was the main focus. For this purpose, we built a robust learning and development platform with an eye on upskilling to develop and motivate them.

- Even more so, we continued to reinforce these through customizing our policies and procedures so that the cause of compassion remains robust and relevant.

3. BUSINESS

Doing business for me was never an accident but a part of my pursuit of impact. It was one platform that, over a period of time, I thought gave me all that mattered to me. In the process of doing business, I kept learning and evolving for the better. Business never put me in a moral fix, as greed was never a factor in my value system. Across its roller-coaster ride, I remained down to earth, powered by strong business ethics. While profit was a goal, it was never to be made at any cost. In my book, I touched upon the business ethics and values that shaped my business journey. I also covered all aspects of business that I self-learned from my failings as well as what I observed from others' failures and success. Being a witness to some extraordinary events of my life between failures and hiccups, I have tried reviewing each with reference to context.

3.1. A Values-Based Organization Is a Fundamental Must

In the course of business and especially in context to organizational realignments, the organization's stakeholders, culture, processes, policies, and procedures must embrace and embed values.

Values, be they honesty, integrity, mutual respect, courtesy, discipline, transparency, compliance, or governance areas, are not a singular driven belief but a force to be reckoned with, one that is to be backed by a collective resolve across all facets of the organization.

Values reflect a company's soul, touching on all its mainstream functions, including the actions of its people. Companies need to ring-fence this by ensuring people with high integrity and moral character are on board with values within the organization and that the company upholds it as gospel. This starts with its leaders, who have to "walk the talk" and become custodians and role models. This creates a culture where values become integral with checks and balances across the company.

Values embodiment must not rest with its CEO alone but with all—the board where shareholders uphold this as the paramount purpose, the CEO who holds the mettle, the C suite that owns it as its guiding force, and the organization mainstream that embraces it as a business continuity need.

I was lucky to have a high moral upbringing, but I only discovered the extraordinary power of values over the years. My life crises did help me in emboldening my values. In my relentless effort to discover myself and in the scrutiny of my actions, these values became my guiding force, as well as the cornerstone of my strategies and relationships. This helped to bring forth a cultural renaissance in all my companies.

Often, I was questioned by my team or people "winking" at my decision to exit client relationships or businesses, as that meant a significant commercial loss to the company or an imminent danger to business continuity. There were many instances where it was my litmus test to uphold what I preached. In one case, with more than $100 million in revenues at stake and a relationship with one of the top ten companies in the world, I had to take the call to exit. It was a matter of respect for my team. Certain individuals were attempting to malign our company reputation, and even more so the morale of our team on the project. I prevailed, and with one push on the button of my notebook, I unilaterally terminated the contract. There was a lot of hue and cry, but in due course our merits prevailed, and after three years the same company awarded us a much bigger portion of their business than before. The moral of the story is truth, and the power of values prevailed. Respect for my colleagues, the company, and myself was enhanced.

At EFS all our relationships, whether with shareholders, employees, clients, or supply chain values, have remained our cornerstone. Policies, procedures, communication, facilities, rewards, and recognition are all administered with a constant reality check on value alignment. The company enforces a corrective culture but not a punitive one. However, there is zero tolerance in regard to moral and ethical fundamentals that uphold fairness and justice.

Reflection Points

- I remained extra cautious that any company policy, campaign, or even handshake must not reflect any departure from company values.

- Having built company values as our key cornerstone, I did not deter from the path those values set out and ensured that everyone in the company also owned it.

3.2. The Company's Strategy and Vision Needs Mainstream Engagement

Every business, whether a small entity or a large public enterprise, needs a vision and mission statement. But unfortunately this is often done more like an afterthought or customary statement rather than a conviction backed by a powerful resolve to achieve your goal. The vision statement provides insight into what the company hopes to achieve or become in the future, and the mission statement communicates the actions that the organization plans to take to achieve it.

Vision and mission are essential prerequisites for starting a business, just like a business plan, feasibility study, capital, and people. In the ordinary course of business, the strategy must align with the company vision, mission, and values. Although I worked in multiple businesses, I've always had a common goal on the positioning, scale, and impact of business. Vision helps to articulate the plan by organizing the necessary resources to move forward. It also needs to factor with whom to benchmark if the business is common to some aspects of that target.

For my first business venture, I crafted a powerful vision backed by my conviction that it would excite all stakeholders. For instance, I positioned Elfina Financial Services as a single-window advisory for high network investors (HNIs) in investments at par with global institutions, a company that was my first venture in the UAE when I had just arrived. This was the first to be licensed by the Central Bank of the UAE in advisory services. It eventually became a provider of preferred choice in a very short time, representing some of the most prominent names, such as Macquarie Group, Fidelity Investments, State Bank of

India (SBI), UTI Mutual Fund, and ING Group, servicing top-notch HNIs in the region with a portfolio of over $1 billion. In the late '90s, Middle Eastern institutions and high network investors were looking eastward, and emerging markets such as China and India were offering interesting investment opportunities in capital markets and related financial instruments.

I saw this opportunity and worked to build partnerships with SBI, UTI, and Software Data (India) Limited, and with Macquarie and Fidelity for Chinese investments. In a short stint, I was able to garner investments of over 1 billion dirhams and placed Elfina among the premium financial companies, competing with some of the global banks. Indeed, here is where vision powered the business plan, and with a team I executed it. The same was true with Wall Street, where I built a company with three countries from a typical exchange house into global transaction services with licenses from the Financial Services Authority, New York Banking Authorities, to the Reserve Bank of India with the first-ever online instant payment platforms.

When I started Kol, my technology enterprise, it was initially envisioned around building a first-ever payment platform to take on big companies like Western Union or MoneyGram International. However, my vision was to build an alternative option that transcended beyond the capabilities of just easing competition and mapping the needs of consumers. I eventually built the most dynamic powerhouse in the region for e-business integration.

When coming to the EFS post and after my tryst with the business debacle of 2008, I was careful in mapping my essential resources, ensuring that people, family, and shareholders were all included in this grand vision: a vision of building a billion-dollar organization through a shared vision, with everyone working together to achieve it.

My vision always encompassed three significant factors: Who do we do business with? What do we do for them? What do we achieve with the value proposition? My answer to this in the context of EFS is that "we work for more than two hundred Fortune 500 companies, as well as the most iconic projects in GCC, with an average engagement period of over five years with over 95 percent retention. We offer seventy-five services across twenty-one countries, and we have, on a combined basis, saved over $300 million across six hundred contracts so far for our clients, in addition to providing high quality and premium end-user experience."

Across five enterprises and business verticals that I built, I consistently achieved the best of credentials, often highlighted by the reputation of those clients, their scale, the precision and complexity of service offered, and the extraordinary great value that I created for them. In this context, I am proud to say that, so far, I have never lowered the bar across all my businesses even in times of having to manage with limited resources. First, my clients were always among the Fortune 500, or the largest in the regions where I operated. Second, all my businesses were cross-border, regional, or international in operations and presence.

EFS and its stakeholders never lost their view on the company vision, and this was well embedded in the core organization through a culture where all owned it. Clients, too, were retained through a unique client engagement program, and our impressive and seamless track record empowered their support to EFS in this vision.

Reflection Points

- Visionary leadership is critical to the business need, much more so than a leader's grandstanding.

- There are three significant factors to operate by: Who do we do business with? What do we do for them? What do we achieve with the value proposition?

3.3. Businesses Need to Adopt Structure, System, and People Alignment

While doing business for two decades until I joined EFS, the concept of people, systems, and structure never came to me as a comprehensive business strategy. The concept of service infrastructure, people, and organizational structure was never focused on. I would look at a business from the standpoint of business development, service offering, profit and loss, and cash flow.

I realized that people, systems, and structure needed to be incorporated to build a resilient business. I ensured that all stakeholders, employees, shareholders, clients, and suppliers' expectations were aligned with the people responsible for the execution. For example, clients need good service delivery; shareholders want a higher and stable return; employees need greater motivation in terms of salary, perks, and work environment; and suppliers wish to achieve the scalability of increasing business.

The company also had issues with its structure between corporate and operations. Most of its shared services were reporting into operating companies and groups operating with fewer controls on operating entities. In essence, the structure added to the woes with too many conflicts. It took me some time, but essentially this move helped me to put all intercompany conflicts to rest.

Surprisingly, there were no International Organization for Standardization standards, technology was invisible, and enterprise resource planning (ERP) ran on a leased platform with negligible management information system (MIS). Systems, too, were not working and had no standards. There was no way to dig for credible data to analyze, as both professionals and the system were incoherent with facts. Therefore, I took some decisive steps with both by bringing in the competence and new ERP systems to back data. There was a long list of reforms and changes that I made.

In just a few months, I took charge of the organization and "rolled heads" to ensure my agenda set in. I also took control of critical clients' portfolios and business development, as I knew I could not have worked on commercial prudence with business scalability on the top of the agenda.

By the close of the first year, I had my stakeholders smiling. The score card was impressive: client retention, 95 percent; employee satisfaction, 87 percent; business growth, 24 percent; and profit growth, 17 percent.

Most of the data was impressive. When I brought the shareholders together for their first-ever meeting, there were grins on their faces. I had delivered on my promise, but I primarily addressed the key challenges in year one in order to start scaling the business without too much disruption.

Every year, we aligned the approach to our core business strategy. In 2011 we introduced the deliverance, prudence, and sustainability model. Businesses were divided between operations, HR, and finance. Most shared services were managed through finance. I institutionalized the role through multiple finance reviews in most sections. I ensured that the business had sufficient checks and balances in all business facets, so all risk management aspects were implemented across most businesses. There were sufficient provisions to maintain commercial prudence across the business, from budgetary controls to MIS.

Technology in the years was the key differentiator, so I delved into every detail to build the business to host under a robust ERP system. Unfortunately, there were too many viewpoints, so I brought a third party in to evaluate the best fit for our needs but also ensured that our visions and needs were aligned when taking a final call. We did it back in 2012; we built full-fledged ERP on Oracle and were awarded by Oracle itself for best implementation.

The list of things to do was endless, so I did not relent facing the many challenges that came my way. By 2013, the company had crossed a contract backlog of $2 billion with net profits growth in double digits. In addition, I expanded operations in fifteen countries and brought a new direction to the business by roping in multinationals to provide IFM service offerings to their regional foothold.

By the end of 2013, we had gained more than one hundred multinationals in the portfolio. These long-term contracts, with good profit margins and strong engagements, helped us scale our business and improve our quality.

In addition, people have been my most significant asset in the making of EFS. In the pursuit of building the company, I must say that I had a select team of professionals from different backgrounds that supported me. They were from other age groups, fields, and ethnicities, but they bought into my proposition. I created a bond where they aligned with my vision, and it became a shared vision.

Who were they? Everyone from the blue-collar workforce to engineers to executives and managers, all roped in together. We built trust by reaching out to them through direct meetings, get-togethers, and events focused on their welfare, not just work. Family values, employees' well-being, and their progression and development were the key aspects of our messaging. People could see us walking the talk and building on the bandwagon of Proud to Be EFSians.

Business in the first three years till 2013 focused on stability and correcting the path to move forward.

Reflection Points

- My business strategy was to ensure risk diversity, and therefore no single contract, country, or business vertical would exceed the acceptable risk diversity standards.

- These considerations would apply across all business aspects, from receivables to suppliers to employees' ethnic mix.

- In later years we transcended this initial goal to encompass many other essentials of diversity.

3.4. Business Scaling Needs Specific Checks and Balances

Business scalability demands that enterprises undertake the adequate scrutiny of their preparedness to manage the upside.

Besides ensuring the availability of requisite factors ranging from commercial viability infrastructure to working capital, this scrutiny must consider a few other parameters from a business-preparedness perspective. Many overzealous entrepreneurs often enter an ambitious business-upscaling mode without adequately assessing essential risks and conducting due diligence. Besides being a critical requirement of growth capital to scale a business, they need to look beyond at other parameters. Technology preparedness is one factor to reckon with, as technology has its scalability limitations, and the company can come to a standstill if the choice of technology is not properly implemented. The competence of people is also a factor that can go awry. Every business level has its specific skill set need, and the team requires that kind of exposure and maturity to ensure that the C suite can manage its growth phase. Enterprise *risk* profile is yet another factor for enterprises to review, as scalability needs to ensure agility. Departing from any of these do's has its implications, so businesses must take cognizance of this.

Review of growth capital is a fundamental requirement in any growth phase, especially in enterprises with previous years of business activity, or those classified as low-profit margin businesses with limited retained capital. The primary source of this growth, equity, can be sourced from shareholders or third-party equity. But as debt, this is mostly not a feasible option, as its cost and repayment schedule makes it unviable.

Entrepreneurs often get overwhelmed by confidence, usually at high points in their business. They go by gut feeling and find themselves in uncharted waters when they enter new businesses. As mentioned earlier, they will often ignore risks and make tall commitments, and managing to fund them becomes a challenge. It is not the venture itself or the decision to make a new business acquisition that is the issue but rather the entrepreneur's disregard of the required due diligence that must be done before jumping on the growth bandwagon. Any quantum growth has its specific mobilization and working capital needs and, in the event of any cash crunch, is bound to be a damp squib.

This also adds to business continuity woes. Being a banker in early life, I saw endless business fatalities due to this. Most SME entrepreneurs are often bowled over due to these issues, not maintaining a balance between their gut feeling and being transported by their passion, emotions, and convictions. Very often, their confident postures overlook the risks of unforeseen events.

In essence, people tend to loosen controls when at their high points, both personal and professional; people do make mistakes. Nevertheless, letting a good business go to waste is not a prudent attribute of a good businessperson. Therefore, all new business leads that could result in a quantum jump need to be closely assessed in regard to the overall company resilience.

Reflection Points

- Business science has taught us about enterprise risk agility.

- Entrepreneurs need to master their foresight by incorporating multiple checks and balances when deciding whether to take any quantum leaps, as ambitious projects must not interfere with smoothly running a business.

3.4.1. PLANNING AND BUILDING A SUSTAINABLE BUSINESS

In any business pursuits, especially in the context of amateurs, the drive to accomplish business goals must not be based on gut feeling and emotions. I continue to see many people with little preparedness embark on entrepreneurial missions. In my early business pursuits too, it never occurred to me to properly plan my ventures or study how to build a business from scratch. It was always some idea with an eye on prospects with a half-cooked strategy that I rushed in those business ventures. I did not follow the prudence logic or the fundamental mantras of doing business. It was in the later years after a series of debacles that I realized that there are essential do's to build. I admit that I made these errors in my life pursuing business where I made wrong assumptions or scaled business without my ability to augment needed financial resources or failed to garner competent people in business. I realized that besides just a business plan, all of these mattered too: commercial scalability and feasibility, deep strategy delving into operations, and financial management.

There is one great misplaced myth that money is the only thing needed to start a business. You may have often come across people saying that without money they just can't proceed, and, in pursuit of this, they tend to ignore the other key requirements needed for starting a business.

What I am trying to emphasize is that money is indeed needed, but that is not the only prerequisite for starting a business, however big or small that may be. For starting a business, one has to have an idea or concept, the resolve to follow it through, the road map, and the resources, both financial and otherwise. An idea is nobody's property, whereas resolve is something that needs to be measured against an individual's own strengths and weaknesses. Questions about mental preparedness, the ability to take risks, overcoming the fear of failure, patience to deal with unforeseen developments, and, above all, belief in one's self should be addressed. I therefore suggest that people, especially beginners, should spend some serious time with themselves before embarking on any business project.

A road map of a business idea is nothing but the business plan. Often, business plans are prepared without undertaking a feasibility study of the proposed business. Actually, a feasibility study is a must for ascertaining commercial viability. Once this exercise is completed and positive conclusions are drawn, only then should the business plan be prepared, thereby defining the objectives, mission, and other management matters.

Last but not least is the financial plan. Remember that this is something that can make or break your business. Follow the golden rule: be conservative with revenue assumptions and generous with expense estimates. Consider various scenarios in the days to come—optimist, modest, and conservative. Evaluate your future cash flow based on the conservative scenario. Check your resolve once again: Up to what extent can you burn your entire capital? If, initially, capital comes through a personal loan, then ensure that cost of finance is provided for. Even if the capital is from your own resources, see how long your cash can hold in the context of a conservative scenario. In the early stages of business, it is advisable to avoid debt, as there would be problems should there be delays.

> Follow the golden rule: be conservative with revenue assumptions and generous with expense estimates.

While preparing for the business, adhere to certain basic business discipline. Business, like any other work, needs commitment, concentration, and consistency, and there are do's and don'ts. Identify related synergies prior to it, moving from the core business to another. Even related diversification should be closely examined prior to any move. I have seen many casualties in start-up ventures due to this, as people tend to lose focus and disseminate their resources. Therefore, leveraging on the given resources is another important aspect to being business savvy. We all have the capabilities to be successful entrepreneurs. What is needed is an organized approach.

A good business start requires thorough due diligence often. Emotions overrule these enthusiasts to embark on a journey that comes with a lot of surprises. Some argue that learning from failures is part of the process, but I say that disregarding basics is foolishness, and such errors do not add to business resilience but instead create unnecessary issues. Remember, ideas and resolve do not make for an excellent business start, but the power of a good business plan with a competent team and adequate resources will; everything matters. I learned that people, systems, and structures all matter to build a sustainable business. Also, one must prepare the company for future uncertainties, as there are always surprises. In my life too, the surprise factor often bowled me over.

After a series of failures, I learned the power of sustainability and then applied it in my business at EFS. In 2012, I introduced a sustainability pyramid focused on my company's business of facilities management. Being a service provider, I introduced deliverance, prudence, and sustainability. Here, I tied the company sustainability to the basic foundation of deliverance, where we were to prioritize robustness in our service offering to our customers, as this was the core of our business offering. I brought in people to ensure higher productivity and an excellence culture through employee motivation and learning. We brought commercial activism and transparency through prudence in our organizational mainstream. We also tied continued learning, innovation, and employee progression to the sustainability segment. These critical deliverance, prudence, and sustainability principles were interlinked, emphasizing service excellence, profitability, and control and continuous improvements.

3.5. Quantum Leaps in Business Growth Need Preparedness, Not Just Prospects

It is every entrepreneur's dream to achieve *quantum leaps* in business. While this of course has its upside, it comes with its own set of challenges and requires apt preparedness of the enterprise itself. Common sense demands that before embarking on any projects with potentially voluminous proportions, it is a must to check vital agility aspects. Any surge will certainly exhaust and create pressure on existing resources, as it will involve all facets of a business, including its people, technology, finance, and infrastructure.

I learned about this mistake and its perils early in my business journey. While building my first venture, Elfina, in the late nineties, I had an ambitious zeal to build a global enterprise. With a great business start and prospects in hand, I, too, moved forward without looking closely at my preparedness for growth. I stumbled and had to face disastrous consequences. This taught me an important business lesson going forward: to be cautious and look closely at balancing growth and business scalability against preparedness.

While preparing for a hoped-for upside, the working capital finance and service infrastructure upgrade can usually be arranged, but other critical do's need more extensive attention. Most vital to this is the company's leadership organization and technology preparedness. This requires more elaborate planning and organization. Any up-front cost that will be offset by future revenues is termed *developmental*. There are various viewpoints on this cost. Financing of a developmental cost is a factor to reckon with, as mapping it with future income is not always easy. Of this cost, the people cost component weighs heavily, and profound insights are required to manage this sensitive balance. In lean organizations with single-digit margins, to provide for such "chicken and egg" developmental costs is not an easy decision for management. Incurring these costs will be a serious problem for the future if growth forecasts fail or fall short.

In my earlier chapters on finance and technology preparedness, I have already discussed the scalability aspects concerning these specific functions. However, in addition to those factors, I would like to emphasize the role of the people-focused organization. In this context, the leadership and its management play a pivotal role in envisioning and execution. They must be prepared to take on the ownership of the company growth bandwagon. Their readiness to do so is paramount to its success and sustainability. Another sensitive issue, especially in mature organizations, is how to manage the chemistry between the incumbent C suite and the addition of new people coming in to support the business upscaling. It is complex and not easy to achieve a seamless induction of new people in the "cozy" setting of its existing C suite. A big challenge is always how to blend the new joiners without leaving existing teams in limbo. Any quantum jump in business requires the company's apex leadership to do a balancing act between existing groups and new joiners across different levels of the organization. This is challenging and often creates a disruption if not managed well. Bringing in new teams requires a well-orchestrated induction process and close engagement, as new people will *not* be thoroughly familiar with the company strategy and culture. At the same time, their incumbent colleagues will have a distinct advantage. These are more likely to be better tuned in with the company's vision, goals, and culture.

However, one more critical aspect that companies must review in quest of this growth phase is their succession planning and progression policies. By far, deep insights of incumbent internal teams are often more valuable due to their experience within the company than insights from the newer teams. The company must ensure the progression of people from within the present ranks to take on the growth phase. If the company has proper performance management and dynamic learning and development programs, it can ensure quicker results. In the EFS context, I was careful to ensure that existing EFSians were appointed to lead the key positions when undertaking new projects, especially the megaprojects. This was primarily achieved through internal career progressions. Progression remained the primary tool of my team's embodiment and motivation. As a result, my C suite has achieved three to four levels of advancement during the past five years, which is genuinely noteworthy.

In context to EFS, I was too caught up with the quagmire of what to do next when I had to move forward with my quantum leap. Having built a lean organization with a high agility factor due to market sensitivities, I was concerned about the capability of my team. I wondered if they could manage the evolving size and dimension of the business, especially as there were specific gaps in the structure. However, I was also conscious of adding new cost burdens by bringing in new people. It took me time, but I carefully articulated this by building a composite suite structure. The incumbent people retained all vertical roles to manage the downstream organization, including the new projects operations. New appointments were primarily made in horizontal positions or in roles that we could not fill through internal progression in the vertical organization. New positions were primarily filled in specialist roles to ensure subject matter expertise to address service excellence or to pave the way for incumbents' progression across the organization, including in new flagship projects. This helped us to retain and promote existing C-suite executives while moving them up the corporate ladder, safeguarding retention and promotion. This ensured that we were able to safeguard the company culture and overall progression in the downstream organization.

Another critical aspect that needs to be addressed before scaling a business is determining the technology that will be employed. This requires strategy and preparedness on many levels. Considering the naturalized life cycle of any sizeable internal technology renaissance exercise, this process involves a minimum of nine to fifteen months. The technology you will need to employ is not something that you can buy off the shelf. Instead, I recommend that the business rethink requirements and plan and map the technology needs. It is crucial to build appropriate technology capability to manage any quantum growth well in advance.

However, the biggest challenge is identifying all the resources businesses need for upscaling, especially the lean organizations with a limited resources pool, and determining how to provide for these resources in advance. This is a huge challenge. I was also at a crossroads when faced with this situation. With auditors at our throats, shareholders seeking higher EBITDA (earnings before interest, taxes, depreciation, and amortization) margins, and banks clamoring for high-interest rates for low-margin business, I had to balance my ambitious growth plan with organizational sustainability. Nevertheless, I managed to earn a historical best ranking in EBITDA of 9 percent and spectacular growth in business, achieving more than double digits.

Reflection Points

- Dreams, grand plans, and ideas do not make success a reality but rather provide a macroreview of the company's SWOT (strengths, weaknesses, opportunities, and threats) analysis.

- First and foremost, a company must have the agility to cope with the impending needs of its growth.

- During this buoyant phase, the stakeholders must map the scalability needs.

3.5.1. BUSINESS GROWTH AND SCALABILITY

Growth and business scalability are some of the bare essentials of business sustainability. Over the years, in the businesses I built, scalability was always integral to my vision. In my journey toward business resilience and the impact I envisioned therein, this remained a critical component of my strategy.

However, I had my own set of challenges in this pursuit, and not all of my ventures achieved the desired results. In my current business at EFS, scalability was indeed my key focus. I wanted to build a USD $1 billion company in ten years and to achieve all other aspects of sustainability with it. For this journey, I built and executed my business plans in short-, medium-, and long-term segments. Initially, in the first year, I concentrated on stability and then moved on to transformation within three years to prepare for my quantum leaps. In 2014, I planned my short, medium, and long terms with definite targets for each phase of reaching my goal. But my first milestone of reaching $300 million in revenues to make a billion-dollar company took longer than I anticipated. I quickly caught up to my original plan, and I was confident of reaching this target within my timeline.

I remained careful in this pursuit not to disregard prudence or sustainability. I achieved the milestones with absolute precision, ensuring checks and balances.

As a storyteller, I stayed the lead in business development. I worked relentlessly on every aspect, from developing relationships, qualitative business submissions, and comprehensive bid engagements to prevail in the process. I was mindful of winning business in all aspects, from engagement to tactical engagements to qualitative bid proposition; everything mattered. I never used the relationship to prevail upon my technical and commercial merits. This remained my biggest strength in my journey, where I was able to meet these tall milestones, just not clenching deals but building a sustainable enterprise despite exponential business growth of compounded annual growth in double digits in the last twelve years.

I not only built a business scale through exponential growth but was able to retain my business. I was successful, as I was able to leverage my skills in intrinsic pricing, deal making, and relationship management.

Across all my leadership roles, I tagged this aspect as part of my key deliverable and demonstrated spectacular business performance. At EFS from 2010 to 2022, I added more than USD $2 billion worth of contracts from iconic projects in the region. I knew that if I had to remain competitive and lean, business scalability was an absolute necessity. With the exponential business prospects in the pipeline and the company's proven track record, I am now able to triple my original vision from $1 billion to $3 billion in the next ten years.

3.6. Transformation Must Not Be Crisis Driven but a Continuous Process

The term "transformation" in the enterprise context refers to a drastic face-lift to people, policy, processes, data, insights, and technology. Its purpose is to address any individual's or organization's change management needs. As a result, it has become a buzzword in corporate circles, with digital transformation occupying the center stage. Moreover, with the COVID-19 pandemic, the need for transformation has become imminent. As a result, it has assumed a colossal dimension with most organizations looking to build resilience with transformational modes to address a series of challenges.

Most wake up to its call when in crisis, while it should instead be a continuous process. It must be encrypted in an organizational introspection mechanism with perpetual assessments and actions. This offers multidimensional benefits and has emerged as a popular strategy tool by management and consultants.

What does transformation entail? A company that fosters teams with transformative mindsets prepared to undertake initiatives of change to deliver desired outcomes. These mindsets and their agendas must be able to override traditional barriers to transform the company.

Technology, innovation, data sciences, and processes are the key allies in most transformation drives. In my work-life history, status quos were never my flavor, as businesses were constantly faced with challenges that made them irrelevant. Especially in my SME ventures, I was always against resource constraints and constantly faced with limitations, and transformation was the only way out. So I never piggybacked on transformation but instead led the transformation and innovation by working to make a cultural shift that everyone would buy into. Everyone worked to support changing the company's mainstream organization, aligning the system and structure to the people.

I also took multiple transformational steps in my life. The first was taking a break to go to Harvard Business School to do my studies midway through life. It was not just about the funding issue but also about taking time out for self-development when I had a family of three to fend for.

> In my work-life history, status quos were never my flavor, as businesses were constantly faced with challenges that made them irrelevant.

It was not an easy decision but was needed, as I just had a graduate degree, and to transcend beyond in the world of finance, Harvard credentials mattered. However, it helped me much more than that, as acquiring these credentials resulted in a monumental change to my personality. I continued my relentless quest for change in my life from then onward. When faced with crises, change remained one of the most prominent pillars of my future actions. In 2003, for example, I decided to enter into a technology venture following my previous fifteen years in finance and banking.

The quest for transformation never left me and remained my ally in my personal and business life, helping me face upheavals and challenges. It always paved the way in my pursuit of making an impact. For instance, in the 2008 crisis, when the world was in turmoil, I, too, was in crisis mode with no resources left for the business to transact. In that situation, it was time for me to assess my transformation through introspection, into the mistakes I made in the industry, and the transition that I had to make to further innovate and reform my business prudence. That transformation mode helped me to achieve business maturity, eventually leading me in my renaissance at EFS and continuing after that.

Reflection Points

- For transformation to take place, first of all, each individual mindset needs to change.

- The individual has to overcome fears and make marked changes in their personality.

3.7. A Concept of Corporate Governance Emboldens Self-Discipline and Disclosures

Most people will relate corporate governance only to large or publicly listed companies, but this must not be seen just in the microcontext but also as a valuable purpose and benefit for any enterprise. It does not matter what size the company is. The basic principles of corporate governance are accountability, transparency, fairness, and responsibility, so it matters to all. Therefore, it is not about the company's size, structure, business, or resources but about setting the rules of engagement for different stakeholders. This must not be feared but respected.

In my journey of working in multiple business domains due to my long history of financial services work, corporate governance remained a critical part of business compliance.

In my initial years in banking, we were warned that any deterrence from adherence to the governance covenants would be a fatal mistake, and these perceptions are misplaced. Unfortunately, these notions often misled people to fear corporate governance. In banking, it is the depositor's interest that requires disclosures and a set decorum.

Because of my early years in banking, I was well tuned to corporate governance. In spite of the small size of my business, I never disregarded management principles. In my partnership interests or joint ventures, I worked tirelessly with my partners to put together elaborate governance, especially on disclosures that matter for partners, bankers, and regulators. I never ignored the provisions of corporate governance, as its guiding principles brought discipline.

In the years of my business transformation and self-reflection, I realized the power of governance and its visible benefits of introspection. In my stint at EFS, where there were more than a dozen operating companies with multiple shareholders, I saw why corporate governance matters and how good governance could help in bolstering shareholder relationships. With my taking over the company in 2010, as I worked tirelessly to improve its framework, my relationship with the board and shareholders skyrocketed in value. The disclosures and their participation through the guidelines outlined in the articles of association helped to strengthen the trust between them and the board. This also allowed the company to improve its risk management strategy and enable improved performance.

In 2014, my company embarked on a preassessment mode to consider the possibilities of going public. We deep dived in detail. That opportunity gave me insights, and that is where I discovered its benefits in building a sustainable enterprise. All those preassessments and due diligence aspects made the organization stronger. They helped bring more excellent controls and disclosures that we may not have otherwise known about. I must say my organization would not have reached this pinnacle if we had not had our guiding principles aligned with our mainstream organization.

Over the last seven years since that exercise, EFS has built a very elaborate corporate governance framework despite limited resources and with no external pressure from outside. Here is where a code of conduct binds all departments and stakeholders, whether it has to do with a board of directors, investor relations, company risk management, or the regulatory framework. The EFS team adheres to it. We don't fear it and have adapted it in our core organizational processes.

During my corporate journey, including ten years at the helm of EFS, my belief that promises or actions cannot deliver results without a strong leader who can make an impact has only been strengthened.

I began to explore ways to ensure that my actions and my team's actions could create transformational results. The concept of corporate governance was seen mostly in context to large corporations and publicly listed companies, as mentioned earlier. Most will connect this to compliances with government regulations and protocols dealing with shareholders' interests. I, however, differ from that micro-objective, as for me, governance is about transparency and the discipline that every organization must maintain with its stakeholders. It is not about shareholders alone but about *all*—employees, clients, bankers, auditors, regulators, and suppliers. Good corporate governance protocols and frameworks ensure outstanding organizational sustainability. None of its requirements interfere with the stakeholders' interests. For instance, good corporate governance emphasizes the need for an independent board and its smooth functioning. The board's role is to help the company run business in tandem with a business plan based on fundamental principles of business prudence. It ensures that no vested interests interfere with the smooth functioning of the company or deviate from the governance framework, risking business or other stakeholders against individual or group interests.

For instance, in the context of shareholder dealings, the board and management have to safeguard majority and minority interests. Board obligations on financial transparency, based on audited statements, assure all stakeholders that the company has maintained a true position of company financial health in regard to all guidelines on that front. However cumbersome these may be, they are actually in the interest of all stakeholders. People in business often complain or overplay the idea that those auditors and regulators are a real "pain in the neck." However, in reality, they help us plug the holes that can be missed in the course of doing business. History shows that some of the largest organizations have failed due to bad governance.

Corporate governance is not just about financial transparency and shareholder dealings but also about legal disclosures, human resources, and business compliance with statutory requirements. Businesses have often been overwhelmed by not complying with these needs, bringing very robust enterprises to risk. I have never lost my attention to the stakeholders' governance in building EFS. I made a conscious effort to identify the different stakeholders clearly. We diligently mapped each stakeholder's needs and then created a governance matrix.

Statutory audits were conducted in absolute transparency as per International Accounting Standards and ensured financial statements represented facts aligned with the vision of the bankers and shareholders. All systems and company procedures would undergo an accreditation process. Also, board management was done strictly in compliance with Articles of Association and regulatory guidelines.

The idea of governance was not to be displayed on the walls as credentials but as tools to learn from the process about how to correct and improve. We would always compare our governance with the previous year's perspectives.

As a business manager and board member in the recent past, I, too, had a tough time dealing with certain corporate governance matters. The toughest in this context was to deal with actions emanating from majority shareholders' interests. Our tactical engagement worked based on our articulated merits of the case.

There were highs and lows, but merits and tactful approaches worked. I forged alliances on the board, communicated well with all stakeholders, and finally prevailed with alignment and composure. I knew there was no room for failure, as the outcome could have been disastrous.

3.7.1. THE ROLE OF THE BOARD OF DIRECTORS, AUDITORS, AND INTERNAL CONTROLS

When analyzing the root cause of any corporate debacle, it is not fair to focus upon the management's actions alone but also to make a holistic review of the firm's "governance ecology," as no outcome can be contemplated without first understanding the structural reasons for the failure.

The roles of the board of directors, internal controls, statutory audits, and regulatory oversights are all components of the governance ecology, and their relative impacts also need to be scrutinized.

How has the board functioned over the years? Were audits conducted? How did the negative results and management misdoings, if any, not come under corporate governance scanners?

Any diagnosis of these outcomes often gets mired in a blame game, which unfortunately takes the focus away from its containment and resolution. These foregone assumptions should be avoided, as they undermine the efforts of stakeholders to contain crises and to apply the learnings from the failings. Wisdom demands that when such events unfold, it is essential for stakeholders to have an unbiased look at the state of the corporate governance regime in a company to identify how these internal controls were circumvented and the compliance framework compromised.

The board must spend some time in introspection on its complacency—if not its failings—should things go wrong. Shareholders usually lay the foundation of robust business management, defining the rules of engagement for the board's structure, mandate, and functioning. For any corporate failure, one must deep dive to see if the board adhered to the governance guidelines and exercised sufficient diligence in management representations. The role of independent directors over the years must also be reviewed, as this significantly strengthens governance. Their independence is imperative to the company's overall interests.

Did the board just follow the formality of ticking the checklist, thereby establishing their own complicity in faulty decision-making? Or did the board function in line with the guidelines in all its deliberations and the decision-making was formalized and recorded?

Reflection Point

- When undertaking a diagnostic review of financial statements, understand the application of the governance policy on the treatment of doubtful/bad debts, compliance with principles of revenue recognition, and potential impairment of receivables.

3.8. Business Resilience Requires an Embedded Risk Culture

It is a common notion that doing business is full of risks. However, I believe it is the entrepreneur's responsibility to discard these fears as much as possible and, without demonizing risk, must learn how best to mitigate it.

The Institute of Internal Auditors defines risk management as "a process to identify, assess, manage, and control potential events or situations to provide reasonable assurance regarding the achievement of the organization's objectives." It is a structured and disciplined approach. It aligns strategy, processes, technology, and knowledge with the purpose of evaluating and managing the uncertainties the enterprise faces as it creates value. It is a truly holistic, integrated, forward-looking, and process-oriented approach to managing all key business risks and opportunities—not just financial ones—with the intent of maximizing shareholder value as a whole.

Risk management is a critical element, like many other essential prerequisites, to be considered before starting a business. In any business plan, we factor in capital needs, a market overview, technology selection and impact, service offering, competition, and risk evaluation. All of this is critically important. The notion of risks can just be assumed on a unilateral basis, and this is where risk management steps in to map and mitigate it.

When we undertake business, we prepare the plan wherein we define the goals and objectives, provide resources, select people, and build a structure to launch business goals. In this, we also evaluate strategic, operational, finance, and compliance risk. Therefore, mapping risks is not a cautious approach but a prudent step toward the sustainability of a business.

It is the company's primary responsibility to blend risk management in the company mainstream, where all stakeholders recognize its vital role. I always give priority to agendas that need to safeguard internal controls, not leaving any room for people to circumvent it. Due recognition is given to flash and internal audits. The company fostered a risk-averse culture where people were educated on the pitfalls of breaches in risk protocols. During audits, the teams were put under intense scrutiny to collaborate, address all concerns, and discard any animosities or negativity.

With the growing need for effective corporate governance, the board and key stakeholders in particular need to be engaged in setting the tone for the priority of controls and risk management throughout the organization. Especially the board and the CEO must step in to take ownership. They must not leave it for their CFOs and auditors but own up to its stipulations. It does not mean that they have to guard their balance sheets or hold them tightly to their chest. As business custodians, they must ensure transparency and factual representation but must not cower down to make compromises about the business prudence due to statutory perceptions, especially those that are not specific to their business. Auditors may have their compliance reasons to push these. Still, companies must speak for themselves to prevail in the interest of all stakeholders.

It is the CEO's job to ensure that core business accounting principles are adhered to while abiding by the direction of International Accounting Standards. The audits must not be feared, nor should its compliance be circumvented in any way. It ensures ideal risk management and a business empowerment process to strengthen business resilience. Often, businesses and finance teams do give in to the pressure of auditors, foregoing critical business considerations. They must not leave it to auditors to maneuver these considerations as per their understanding unless there are strong reasons to do so. These misconstrued judgments often emanate from a limited knowledge of the business model itself.

It is a typical scene to see a tug-of-war played out between the auditors and finance team. This annual squabble between the auditors and companies, though short lived, is familiar to most audit engagements. This fracas mostly occurs regarding the treatment of income and expense statements by the company and the audit objections therein. Both sides seem to squander whatever they can on either side, entrenching their positions, be it revenues, treatment of expenses, income recognitions, or receivables aging.

There are endless aspects where the auditors and finance do not see eye to eye, and with the advent of technology, new algorithm-based analytics, and strengthening of International Financial Reporting Standards, auditors are looking to execute more extensive scrutiny. The audit activism is putting a lot more onus on businesses for financial transparency. However, this merits a proper interpretation of risks and not just hollow perspectives as to the risk category. These usual business risks are common to business essentials, and provisions such as the expected credit loss (ECL) ratio are to be applied wherever needed, not as a blanket application to all businesses. The ECL provisions have now become a severe bone of contention, as auditors want to have a minimum number for their compliance with accounting standards.

For instance, the COVID-19 pandemic is an extraordinary phenomenon that has had a macroimpact. Still, its risk assessment is carried out on the business's macroaspects and microaspects. Auditors, while reviewing such risks, must understand the real business impact instead of the standard provisions and draconian obligations on all to adhere to. Auditors need to develop a mechanism to differentiate business risk based on the industry and the specific business profile of the company.

The recent corporate debacles in the region have indeed put the onus on auditors to exercise extra care while studying balance sheets. But that does not mean this fear-mongering on corporate governance should wreak havoc on the company balance sheet. The audit activism only puts businesses at a higher risk, leaving the companies with bloated balance sheets sitting on undue provisions.

I fully endorse that businesses have to exercise due caution in presenting an accurate picture with evidence of tangible facts on various provisions. I agree these need to be given transparent disclosures, and CEOs need to lead the process with full engagement. However, auditors also need to strengthen their diligence approach with transformative measures.

To ease the usual scuffle that is played out on this turf, both sides have to follow a better engagement procedure. The companies must first get an updated charter of the audits with inclusions of new accounting provisions so that the company team may study this in advance and hold internal workshops to ensure that the auditors are provided with proper formats. In addition, the two must hold prior seminars to address the "housekeeping"

> The company's CEO must be integral to some of the critical milestones rather than just huddled down, signing the balance sheets.

issues, as these remain a deterrent for a smooth process. The company's CEO must be integral to some of the critical milestones rather than just huddled down, signing the balance sheets.

It's time for both sides to take their respective audit roles and responsibilities more seriously. The audit companies need to bring competent professionals, article assistants, and interns with a thorough understanding of the process and the business itself. The managers and the partners need to rise to the challenge of building more robust diligence based on insights from credible industry data, instead of just a few handpicked ones of their own. These have to engage all the stakeholders across the full process and not just meeting for a handshake. To sum up, the regulators, too, have to wake up to the reality of the audit woes. It is time to define a mechanism on how audit firms conduct audits and adhere to the minimum qualification criteria for audit professionals and the process therein. By bringing this to the table, auditors can also help in promoting corporate governance by conducting a period risk assessment and by analyzing the whole risk tolerance of the company and the efforts that the company has made toward lessening the risk.

3.8.1. THE PROSPECTIVE ROLE OF AUDITS

An independent audit provides another corporate governance limb to safeguard companies. This process seems to have been strengthened with the enforcement of International Accounting Standards promoting transparency and standardized disclosures. However, a fundamental issue remains.

There is a need to move away from the practice of a random sample approach and instead employ forensic tools to ensure closer scrutiny of large ticket transactions in balance sheets. Audits need to take a saner view of how the company's management has treated the key accounting provisions that can have material impact on financial statements. In some of the recent corporate failures, this aspect has been called into question. This can easily be avoided if the audits adopt appropriate caution. Auditors must seek satisfactory explanation to the various provisions and ensure any concerns are directly discussed with the audit committee and/or at board level.

The internal audit must rise above controls to ensure the accounting rises above bookkeeping and balancing to fundamentals of prudence. Regulators have the power to establish rules of engagement, monitor compliance, investigate breaches, and make recommendations to penalize offenders in both a corporate and personal capacity.

Reflection Points

- The role of the regulator oversees that the whole of the corporate governance function is an important player for the safeguarding of shareholders.

- The role of internal audits is often understated, although it should be the one raising the red flag at an early stage of any corporate disaster in the making, not to necessarily review them in a whistleblower role but to ensure the management follows due processes.

3.8.2. LEGAL CLARITY AND UNDERSTANDING ARE MUSTS FOR BUSINESS REQUIREMENTS

Companies and businesspeople must have a thorough understanding of their enterprise risks, especially its primary risks, and these must be factored in before taking any actions. Prior to outsourcing this to lawyers or legal counsels, they must evaluate the pros and cons. Like many critical aspects in business, legal risks are a critical component, though I believe these are part of any common sense and logic and must not be complicated. In reality, though, most people put this for a lawyer's review, as they think it is out of their reach. Primary or secondary legal checks are the way to mitigate risks connected with the business's legal structure and its contractual dealings with others and provides a sanity check of the compliance risks. I recommend that both a self-review and a lawyer's review are essential, but they cannot be left for later.

The world of jurisprudence seems complex, but if you follow the fundamental ethics in business and streamline your business discipline through checks and balances, you are likely to face the least turbulence. However, it would be best if you mapped your risks based on your business profile by building a comprehensive risk register. A good business must delve into details to put comprehensive checks and balances in place to build robust risk mitigation in its mainstream organization.

The evolving models of business necessitate a complete change in the conventional business mindset, from setting a mere strategic business plan and the commercial parameters to achieve the plan to a more blended approach whereby any strategic plan won't be successful enough without giving full consideration to the legal aspect of the business (internal/external). The road to create a successful organization and risk mitigation process starts from the level of legal knowledge of the management before engaging experts from law firms whose role, generally, will be limited to reducing your legal plans and thoughts into clear documents or actions that reserve the rights of the business. The idea is simple, as understanding the legalities of your business and its environment is a robust tool for the law experts to sculpt the required legal understanding of your organization into a compliant and seamless system.

3.9. Laying the Foundation of Business Prudence

My realization of the importance of business prudence did not come to me as a business management lesson but with the adverse outcomes of my decisions, both personal and professional. For instance, when I was just twenty-six years old, I went to put a down payment on a house with zero cash in hand in anticipation of funds that would come through company loans. With no clear indication of this and just on expectation, I went on to make a huge financial commitment. This led me to a lot of hardship to clear up that mess. I made mistakes, though these were not due to gambling or speculative purposes. I was ambitious and would take risks, often not factoring in unlikely outcomes that would change the course of the results. Driving businesses with tall agendas was always my objective, but my business plan would not always fit in the feasibility assumptions for various reasons. It could be because of market conditions or internal shortcomings. Prudence therefore teaches you that business has its risks and helps you to measure its impact and prepare to respond by managing or mitigating it.

I got to know the meaning of prudence over the course of business during my initial years of stepping up as an entrepreneur, but I did falter, making many wrong moves. Making decisions based on a gut feeling and superficial assessments without assessing the true pros and cons is often where young entrepreneurs go wrong. Having been through those nightmares, the learning process I underwent guided me to cut losses and find ways to build resilience. To be prudent means applying foresight, and being farsighted as well, to measure risks, assimilate scale, and ensure outcomes with the least possible downside. Utilizing the concept of a prudent organization, we can build a culture where opportunities are mapped with given resources and related risks. Commercial opportunities are weighted based on given resources within the gamut of business scale and capability as part of the cost provided for businesses while also factoring in unforeseen risks.

EFS as a company and business did give me my launching pad as a businessman, as I learned to master the art of business resilience after a three-year grueling period of struggle in my past businesses. I was ready, just out of the furnace, so to speak, so I started by laying the right foundation. I laid the rules of prudence by making the businesses centered around business finance with risk mitigation but not control. The world of commercial prudence was made integral to operations and business sustainability. In other ways I financialized the operations model to enable people in operations to understand the intrinsic cost of their operations and to map their incomes to show their incurred costs. The idea was to show people in operations why it was important to manage their budgets and understand the basic concepts of profitability.

We embedded prudence in department and individual KPIs. We then outlined the key aspects of prudence around contract management, budget, MIS, cash flow, compliance and audits, bookkeeping, and supply chain sourcing, defining what was best suited to our business model and industry dynamics.

Resilience and prudence are actually the same sides of a coin. In business, the term "prudent" matters.

Having learned the game of applications and uses of funds in my previous businesses and how poor cash flow management can ruin businesses, I was greatly intrigued when I came on board at EFS. I realized that the EFS businesses had all their resources caught up in providing for capital expenses, new expenses, and receivables. There was no working capital left over. The company had zero debt, with all capital stuck in business with no free cash flow. Management was busy making decisions on capital expenditure, new expenses, and business growth with wafer-thin margins. Continuing pilferage of monies in expenses and stuck-up cash in receivables had brought the business to its knees.

The company so far thrived on owners' capital alone with no access to debt for working capital. The concept of revenue and expenses is not a matter of profit and loss only but that of cash flow to weather the outflows or inflows that are in accordance with business cycles. We had most monies employed in applications like selling, general, and administrative expenses (SG&A) or cost of sales expenses, not even in asset-backed investments, and those, too, were much more than any requisite standards. This was clearly indicative of a lack of commercial prudence and a lack of leadership foresight on the fundamental principles of prudence.

If business is to proceed beyond normal strategies, it also requires boosters. Every year we shall identify a certain strategic push to push specific agendas, from revenue optimization to productivity purge to innovating ideas. Back in 2010 we first launched our system structure and people to ensure overall organizational revival, and then in 2012 we embarked upon excellence and commercial prudence and sustainability as a way to balance between operational excellence and our commercial objectives.

In the last five years, at EFS we launched multiple annual campaigns with specific areas of focus. Our campaign ELATE was the company's push to build an efficient, lean, agile, tactical, and effective organization. Then in 2019, IOT—innovate, optimize, and transform—was to transform company cost optimization and then in resilience transformation tactical in 2020. This was to build a resilient culture with emphasis on transformation and a tactical mindset. These campaigns helped us to bring the team together with great ideas as well as definitive strategies.

SME businesses need to have continuous drive to innovate business strategies to raise revenue, improve margins, and eliminate inefficiencies. There cannot be room for conformity. In the backdrop of lean resources, these SMEs have to rise above to meet challenges.

Reflection Points

- In my life, after going through a difficult journey of ups and downs, it was my tryst with prudence that made me worldly wise. I learned how to navigate it but still have not mastered it.

- I believe no one has yet been able to completely master prudence. Business prudence requires a scrutiny of all associated known risks, and to an extent it can be achieved and will always have a mitigating effect on them.

3.10. Technology and Innovation

3.10.1. COMPANIES MUST EXERCISE CAUTION WHILE UNDERTAKING AMBITIOUS TECHNOLOGY PROJECTS

Businesses of any size cannot afford ambitious commitments based on sheer enthusiasm. CEOs and the companies' IT leadership must apply caution while deciding on in-house technology advances.

A company must only consider IT projects based on a strong business case, wherein all the merits of such projects are mapped out and all other prerequisites complied with.

It is not just the need and cost that matter or the fact that it's unavailable as an off-the-shelf application. The decision to go for an in-house initiative has to be based on much more comprehensive scrutiny. There must be full preparedness of the company's ecosystem and all other critical fundamentals of the software life cycle development process to roll out such projects.

I continue to see management under pressure from their units citing compelling business needs and rushing into hurried software developmental engagements. Many a time, the management is cornered to take hasty decisions by overenthusiastic tech-oriented individuals and teams.

Companies, therefore, often enter into hurried developments without going through a full review of the business capability in terms of its implementation, scalability, and obsolescence.

Some Basic Steps

Before embarking on any in-house development or purchase of a product, there needs to be a detailed process, including the full involvement of the board of directors and the technology committee, to review such decisions. This process must not only include business mapping needs, functionality, and cost reviews but also include its implementation program, technical and application scalability specs, and obsolescence factor. Third-party consultants should also review the program or make use of resources such as Gartner reviews.

While externally led tech offerings have the expertise and credibility to support all aspects of software development, internal ERP needs to have all the processes and competencies critical to roll out successful in-house IT applications.

In this context SMEs, in particular, must exercise extra caution, as they will have to allocate precious resources needed to manage these.

Over my long years of working in corporate management, I have seen millions wasted on rushed IT developmental projects that did not see the light and many that were not implemented effectively.

A Sheer Waste of Resources

The fundamental issue here is a faulty envisioning process or bad implementation due to a lack of preparedness. It is a common sight to see stalled IT projects. This may not be as common to ERP applications, as this needs deeper scrutiny from management, and the decision-making process is more comprehensive due to higher budgets.

However, for front-end and middleware applications, there remains a challenge. Understandably, each business struggles to have its specific functionality needs met, and those that can't find solutions from standard applications have to work on other options.

The choice is to either develop an app in house or to seek a third-party app. However, this process needs an exact and well-managed strategy and plan. It is quite common to see companies with a number of overzealous IT applications throughout their development history that they could not use or realize the full impact thereof.

These misguided overtures are not just about missed opportunities but instances of colossal waste. These investments not only impair balance sheets but undermine the digital resolve of the company.

Reflection Points

- Most management cannot necessarily evaluate the merits of IT applications, as it is outside of their range of expertise, but instead will need third-party inputs to provide holistic guidance.

- The process of evaluation between in-house and outsourcing requires all proposed IT applications to go through financial scanners in order to ensure they will be able to serve the required purpose in the most effective manner.

3.10.2. GUARDING AGAINST TECHNOLOGY-DRIVEN OBSOLESCENCE

Rising costs can no longer be an excuse to keep outdated platforms in use for longer than they are viable. Businesses have been struggling for too long due to technology obsolescence and the treatment of these investment provisions in their balance sheets. This colossal waste of money has management and auditors embroiled in continuous deliberations on how to manage these disruptions.

This has become a bone of contention between auditors and the management when reviewing company balance sheets. Reflecting on the merits of these concerns, it is essential for business leaders to understand tech obsolescence issues and safeguard businesses against their fallout. This needs to mitigate impaired investments swelling on the company's books.

Bloated assets with difficult-to-ascertain viability and mapping of their business gains are constant challenges in balance sheets these days. Management needs to take proactive measures before making investments in new tech applications to mitigate obsolescence risks.

It is crucial to carry out in-depth reviews of current needs and future scalability in line with the emerging industry landscape. The selection process must include a third-party review and be done to ensure an optimal return on investment (ROI).

It is imperative that holistic reviews are done and that management is not hoodwinked by sales propositions from service providers. In my own experience, I have seen in more than two instances during a development period of eighteen months that technology costs were written off due to inordinate delays in project implementation, and an alternative had to be introduced due to changes in requirements.

One can imagine how such write-offs impact balance sheets. Considering the current technology headwinds, business leaders must try to use clear foresight and ensure their tech investments, licensing, maintenance, and implementation costs are both productive and sustainable.

Owners should also safeguard capital assets from obsolescence by outfitting their businesses with leased equipment versus purchasing the items outright. By adopting this approach, the company is free to upgrade to new technology at the end of each lease or include a provision that allows for technology trades.

Technology specification is a fundamental construct that includes considerations such as database design, architecture, and hosting framework. These decisions must not be left to CTOs and consultants alone and should be well within the radars of CFOs and CEOs too.

These are critical factors for future scalability, as they can lead to functional logjams that would eventually seed further obsolescence. Audits are useful instruments that should be used to assimilate risks for calibrating tech-related budget planning.

The rapid pace of development of new generation software and hardware should not be underestimated before making technology investment decisions. If organizations want to be sustainable, they will need to reflect and take action on mapping issues, as we all know that obsolete software can drain valuable organizational resources like an infestation of termites.

Developing a long-term strategy for automation is critical, and it is imperative to have a technology sustainment plan, including allocation of full-time internal and external resources. An effective mitigation strategy starts with a long-term view of the challenges as well as management of change. The plan should be linked to the overall strategy with a five-to-ten-year outlook.

Patent information should be used as guiding principles for the development of proactive obsolescence management at every stage of the product life cycle with clarity on end of life and/or end of support.

Reflection Points

- An effective obsolescence management process must be put in place as an integral part of the organization's software and systems life cycle management.

- This entails the upkeep of inventoried databases of the components in use and how they should be managed throughout their life cycle.

3.10.3. HOW TECHNOLOGY HAS ENABLED POSITIVE PROGRESS BOTH DESPITE AND BECAUSE OF COVID-19

Amid the ongoing trauma that the market is facing, there are indeed traces of positivity. In this turmoil, there is a glimmer of hope on many fronts, and technology is indeed leading that positivity. One wonders, Where is this sudden transformation coming from, and what are the critical drivers pushing this agenda? The change of mindset has influenced the recent technology renaissance that people have embarked upon. Today, business stakeholders are all eager, more than ever before, to get on the bandwagon.

Surprisingly, the technology has been there for some time. However, with new transformative mindsets, people have adopted technology solutions as part of their routine. For instance, Zoom, Microsoft Teams, and various other telephony platforms have been there for some time. Still, only limited businesses were holistically using these. Many of these solutions were in waiting to be a part of the mainstream organizations, but the current emergence of these technologies and their adaptation has been spectacular. As per a Chinese proverb, there is an opportunity in every crisis. Indeed, this is true; during COVID-19 times, technology definitely has been walking the talk. The meteoric rise of technology often enters the discussion as a way to ensure core business restitution.

In the business of facilities management, for example, tech has arrived with a big bang. From management functions to operations, all roles are riding on this wave of technology transformation. The management's and project teams' time and monies that used to get wasted on meetings, logistics, and movement of the executives are now being managed more productively. These are proving to be a big boon for businesses. These have not only helped in time efficiency but have given a push to process optimization by helping to record and organize meeting notes. In our company, we have been holding two out of three interactions through teams that have considerably eased demands on our executives. This has given them a boost to better leverage their time to address operational issues.

Having been back 100 percent at the workplace for some time at our company, we are in for a stark realization of the power of IT and how it is transforming our business with these new applications. We see how these solutions are helping the organization with employee productivity and cost optimization. While project teams can now concentrate on their project supervision and are available to give more quality time to their clients and groups, at the same time, finance is happy to see lower travel and logistics costs. The same is the case with corporate and board experience using this new telephony. During the lockdown and with social distancing, we were able to hold all our quarterly meetings through these tech telephony platforms. One can't imagine the cost benefits of such a change.

The various new systems and applications are quickly changing the FM executives' routines with more productive outcomes. For instance, the new age computer-aided facilities management (CAFM) systems and mobile apps are helping executives and field teams to monitor live operations through dashboards and webcams. These provided critical information to manage off-site supervision and surveillance through live dashboards during the COVID-19 crisis, and its compliances have pushed the industry to think beyond and have aligned FM in express technology mode.

The visitor's management system is helping to ease the pressure on front desks as well as helping to meet the new COVID-19 compliances on social distancing. Likewise, many other applications from space to document management are now in place and are making significant strides, which is not only helping in streamlining and consolidating processes but also helping with better time management. Tech is now embedding itself for most FM professionals. In particular, the FM industry with its wafer-thin margins is riding on this wave of transformation to achieve cost efficiencies in administrative time management across various segments, from resource deployment to document and project management processes.

In the wake of this crisis, FM also bore the brunt with falling revenues and rising costs. FM was on the back foot, and the industry had no option but to transcend their previous level of efficiencies. This labor-intensive industry has also helped to sustain its workforce's engagement and welfare through technological nuances to communicate using a broad reach through multimedia.

The COVID-19 pandemic has been the driver that has brought in such mass digital and tech transformation like never before. Like the rest of the businesses, technology is indeed playing a pivotal role. It is serving the long-standing needs of FM in terms of lean and efficient resource management. These have kicked in with definitive efficiencies in cost that has helped in easing the pressure where the industry is no longer seen as a behind-the-scenes player but as an industry that provides agile and faster solutions along with greater transparency.

Reflection Points

- The advent of new technologies empowers the day-to-day life of a facility manager.

- These are revolutionizing operations both in terms of process optimization through the telephony platform and CAFM optimization supported by tool and machine automation.

3.11. Learning and Development

3.11.1. CORPORATE L&D NEEDS TRANSFORMATIVE CHANGES TO ACHIEVE GOALS

The corporate learning and development (L&D) landscape is changing fast. It requires deep introspection, especially in context to mounting challenges that businesses are facing. There is an imminent need for change. A paradigm shift is the need of the hour to step away from the traditional approach, moving away from training regimes to holistic learning and development.

Having been engaged in various L&D engagements, I see a strong business case for transformation. L&D proponents have to lead with mettle to create an innovative and digital revolution in this arena.

I believe that there is a significant disconnect between the actual needs of executive learning and the way conventional L&D organizations are working. We have to overcome the traditional fixation with training and its assessment methodologies. The new age human resources development systems are still not addressing the actual needs. The L&D needs of the organization are done more as a checklist of "things to do" rather than as an automated assessment criterion that comes directly out of performance management.

> A paradigm shift is the need of the hour to step away from the traditional approach, moving away from training regimes to holistic learning and development.

Companies' emphasis is often driven from a brand-building perspective or as a marketing pitch to clients. Most trainings are awarded as trophies, as a reward and recognition method, or as an employee motivation tool rather than as professional development based on embedded assessment criteria.

Why is there a lacuna? Is this due to a lack of corporate strategy or the leadership engagement itself? For the success of L&D, the organization needs to embed professional development as a critical pillar in its mainstream organization where all leadership levels are engaged. It then has to build systems and tools to identify and assess employees through state-of-the-art performance management systems that outline L&D outcomes. These outcomes must catapult the employee's performance across personal, professional, and functional capabilities. The performance management system through smart KPIs must differentiate between skill gap and progression capabilities so that a fair assessment is done between correctional and developmental areas.

Robust technology platforms are required to help aid HR and operation managers to manage the assessments and then work with the L&D organization to identify the needs. Based on these assessments, the company's L&D departments have to develop course curriculums based on blended learning. The traditional instruction-based class learning needs to reinvent itself. The most significant portion of executive learning must come from being on the job. However, to achieve the maximum impact of on-the-job learning, the role of field mentors becomes a must. They must be able to provide dynamic and apt guidance for on-the-job training schedules. Also, the online learning process will need to be an integral part of the course curriculums, without which full impact cannot be realized. L&D can serve a better purpose with a new blended approach of 20:50:30, where 20 percent is based on instructional, 50 percent is on the job, and 30 percent is on self-learning or online learning.

To deliver such a dynamic approach and shift in the organization policy, this has to be a shared goal and not only a CEO's wish list. At EFS, we realized this need well in advance. We have tried addressing all three aspects from assessment and course development to their execution through state-of-the-art course management. It is hosted on an innovative IT platform that is linked to each element of L&D.

Reflection Points

- Besides building HR development systems on performance management for assessment, companies must also invest in a dedicated L&D organization, with in-house faculty who are competent to develop and run relevant curriculums.

- Such setups will also need education management systems that can successfully administer these programs.

3.11.2. BUSINESSES MUST GO BEYOND CONVENTIONAL ON-THE-JOB TRAINING TO MAKE IT HAPPEN

There is much activism now about training at most workplaces. Private and government organizations have been factoring in how best to leverage its impact. These are not just postures but are occurring due to a heightened awareness influenced by many factors.

The conventional approach to training is transforming. There are evolving narratives on how to strengthen the developmental aspects of training, and experts continue to devise strategies to achieve this. There seems to be a unilateral conclusion that effective training guarantees productivity and stronger engagement, as well as assures financial efficiencies.

New generation training regimes are being delivered, which involve interactive workshops, games, and group participation with the support of tech aids. The ongoing transformation is helping, but still, the entire approach needs a face-lift. The new phase of training is shifting its focus from business continuity and excellence to that of being a critical business-empowering tool.

Belated Wisdom

This is indeed a welcome awakening, as more organizations adopt it as a matter of necessity. While establishments have started realizing the benefits, addressing the highest priorities first, it still needs a robust corporate push.

There is a visible resistance to prioritizing training on top of the business's agenda. Forget the tokenism of renaming departments as "L&D." L&D has to be integral to a company's core organization strategy with full engagement of its C suite and each of its departments.

The current business climate is also not helping. There is a lot of resistance about the cost factor. Businesses are torn between how to budget for training costs against the waning bottom line, as well as negate its treatment on their books. Should this cost be treated as an overhead or as a developmental expense?

The notion is that it is a "developmental cost" that helps businesses to reduce costs through a productivity boost and related efficiencies. Nevertheless, the establishment is finding it difficult to provide for it amid falling margins. It is, therefore, time to engage sceptics to highlight the 360-degree benefit of training and bring in more believers to make training a business sustainability tool.

Management needs to adopt the L&D strategy and move away from traditional training and insipid corporate engagements. Businesses need more interactive learning tools and machine learning.

The C suite has to embrace L&D as a mainstream need with specific calendars that are fully integrated with corporate strategy.

Reflection Points

- Training must not be engaged only as a hopeful motivational boost.

- Its assessment must be based on the review of an individual's SWOT analysis and the company's desired goals that will be impacted by that employee.

- The new learning approach must empower individuals and teams to transform their personal and professional goals and not just exist as a ruse to escape the workplace!

3.11.3. BUSINESSES MUST GET CRACKING WITH UPSKILLING

Businesses are looking at all available options to managing their risks as a result of the ongoing slowdown and the resulting chain of uncertainties. This is not enough, as the need is to move away from defensive postures to transformative leaps. This needs to be done to remain in resilient mode. The business case of upskilling must get its due priority. It was long overdue and all the more so in the current context. With job losses soaring, the case of upskilling and reskilling will need a strong push at every level.

There are significant efforts required at the governmental level to intervene to review structural labor dynamics. The need is to do a deep dive into ways to reskill and upskill the labor force through reforms to address long-standing anomalies.

An upskilling push can apply to all, and this is nothing short of an emerging necessity. From manufacturing to services to desk jobs, there are varying needs to meet objectives of productivity, tech advances, and tool automation, as well as a rising demand for technical skills across industries. The construction, building maintenance, and logistics categories have long been demanding a skills upgrade.

It wouldn't be amiss to start doing so now, given that cost-cutting and productivity surges are ruling business agendas. Upskilling and reskilling are becoming critical tools to optimize costs.

What Will Separate Winners from Losers

Upskilling ensures that the workforce has adopted new tech ways, leading to efficiencies and, of course, reduced headcount costs where needed. Post-COVID-19, this will be the differentiator for companies, as the right mix of human resources and process automation efficiency will drive resilience. With the emergence of new communication needs and machine automation, upskilling is primed for takeoff.

While this requires whatever investments can be diverted short term, it will eventually ensure business continuity. Considering the current cash flow situation, such provisioning may be difficult. But however hard it may be, businesses have to get innovative on cost allocations and provide for this.

Think beyond Redundancies

As an extension of corporate social responsibility, businesses have to minimize job redundancies wherever possible through reskilling across its workforce. Companies opting for layoffs have to be mindful of the "true" cost of staff cuts. While it may not serve the purpose of overall cost reduction, avoiding higher layoffs can be beneficial for all.

Get On with It

Companies have to fast-track upskilling through one- to three-month programs that emphasize self-learning and online support, which would also reduce the cost of engaging a third party. It has to be backed by sweeping changes to internal culture, with the leadership actively involved in making that transformation.

There are multiple ways to connect upskilling costs to ROIs as well as mapping direct financial benefits to employees.

Companies that can implement a complete upskilling program stand to benefit in the long term.

Reflection Point

- Employees need to be engaged in upskilling as the next step toward their professional development and not just as a means to ensuring job security.

3.12. Role of Finance as a Business Enabler and Partner

In doing business and learning its do's and don'ts, I was cautious to remove the perception of finance as a control function. In my humble understanding, finance is a business enabler. It is not to be feared or hated but embraced as a business partner. Its role as a custodian of risk is to safeguard business interests.

Finance has its functions split between business finance, risk treasury, and accounting, and each has its own specific objectives. Therefore, we emphasized each purpose, and when putting together the business structure, we ensured that finance had covered all facets of the businesses and their touchpoints.

For instance, a budget, a vital tool to manage business, has its needs and requires all to adhere to a discipline. While business owners have the primary responsibility to manage budgets, finance must ensure that people adhere to discipline. To achieve this, I ensured that organizational culture develops respect for processes and compliance and adopts risk culture as an owned attribute, not only as accountability.

People are always concerned about my fixation with a financialized corporation where financial perspective from commercial leverage was the objective, though not from a control perspective. The power of such a matrix was to ensure that the concepts of prudence and entrepreneurship prevail. Its results were astonishing, as in the case of EFS over the last thirteen years. Our results are a reflection of how finance as a tool of prudence can benefit the organization.

These remained critical to business sustainability prerequisites. We ensured that all stakeholders in our business mutually accepted these without a hue and cry about these processes, in order to support the mutual objective of the organization. We prevailed in ensuring that all departments, including operations and finance, mutually worked together to build robust outcomes with these checks and balances. We made sure all involved were able to introspect on various dispute resolutions and outcomes to build a culture of "learning from mistakes."

Prudence and risk need a balance, but putting one over the other is not the right approach, and I carefully isolated these perspectives from my financial organization.

In our organization today, most stakeholders consider finance as a close ally in their business continuity needs and will vouch for their role as a partner and enabler, not as that of a controller.

Best practices laid the rules of engagement for finance in running businesses. Each of its functions plays a pivotal role in business sustainability. However, I would like to elaborate on specific tasks like bookkeeping, cash flow, and debt to revenue and cost recognition, where specific roles of these functions need the attention of business owners for a better understanding.

3.12.1. BOOKKEEPING, COST PROVISIONS, REVENUE RECOGNITION, AND PROJECT AND ACCOUNTING WORKS

Accounting integrity and discipline are essential to the character of any finance organization. All must ensure that an accurate picture of company income is provided in books where accuracy and timeliness both matter. Ensuring all cost provisions and revenue recognition must be done as per acceptable accounting standards and best business practices in context to that business. For instance, all sales costs from employees' end of service benefits to material costs plus overhead are provided, irrespective of whether current or deferred should be fed into the system every month, including overhead. There should be no attempt to underprovide for costs and map it directly to revenues booked. It is common practice in business circles to defer providing for certain expenses to inflate profits, and vice versa, and booking certain revenues that do not meet the merits as per accounting practice or are not certified by the client.

Besides the other risk parameters of governance and statutory compliance, the window dressing of accounting is one of the most significant challenges that many companies face when accounting books are compromised. Therefore, in accounting, timely booking and maintenance of books are very critical, and accounting risk functions like reconciliation, third-party confirmation of balance, end of services actuary evaluation, and receivable aging are all important steps to adhere to and require scrutiny from management, auditors, and the board of directors.

3.12.2. DEBT MANAGEMENT—BUSINESSES NEED TO REIN IN THEIR DEBT

Debt plays a vital role in any business. It is a necessary evil you cannot avoid, and you must know how to manage it. Debt fills the void between available capital, what we call owner funds and requisite funds needed to meet the business needs. It is not simple, as many aspects should be considered when evaluating the quantum and timing of debt.

What is good debt, and what is bad debt? Yes, it matters. Short-term debt with an agreed repayment timeline but not on demand with low interest, which is aligned to what the business can afford in terms of cost, is considered good debt. As per the business cash flow cycle, any long-term debt with market-aligned interest and tenor is good debt. At the same time, a debt could become a bad debt if carrying a high-interest rate and with payment terms that do not align with business cash flow.

Debt refers to all borrowed monies, so don't mistake that this refers to only bank loans or loans from others, but it includes all types of borrowings, including family loans, supplier credits, and unpaid bills.

Businesses need to carefully take a reality check on the needs and take a saner view of the business ability to repay the debt based on its quantum, cost, and tenor.

How must businesses, especially SMEs, plan their debt needs? This is based on their ability to map between applications and uses of the funds versus the deficit, if any, and must take cognizance of its cash flow assessments. It is not the profits alone that must set the basis of debt but also its quantum, tenor, and the cost of debt no matter what the source is. There are defined ratios with some maximum ratio indicators that should ideally not be more than 1:2 debt to equity as a norm. Often in mature businesses, these might vary. Still, wisdom demands that debt ratio must also see the business's ability to repay within the allowed tenor, and at times low margins or losses might impair the capability to repay. Also, the working capital debt must not be more than 120 days of business revenue, or aligned to the receivables cycle, and assuming that receivables aging is contained within a reasonable period. Working capital-related debts must only be taken against receivables collaterals, while capital-related debt, if not heavy plant and machinery, should be repaid within three to five years maximum. Debt repayment must not be earmarked against future cash flow, profits, or new debt but should be paid from earned free cash flow and profits.

Efficient debt management requires a sound financial discipline and a prudent culture where stakeholders understand the ills of bad debt management. It requires businesses to carefully understand its drawbacks in the event of its failure and manage it within the allowed norms. An SME, in particular, needs to make a prudent debt management pledge. He or she must follow this as a gospel where quantum, timing, cost, tenor, source, and ratio are essential factors.

Global norms for enterprises suggest that the maximum ceiling is three times EBITDA. Still, some may argue, citing each business has its specific needs and guiding principles, but none must cross the red line of debt-equity ratio and free cash flow.

In my own business journey, I have seen how the ills of poor debt management can affect the business survival of day-to-day businesses. The mistake I made in the past was connecting debt to foreseeable profits in the business alone but not taking into account the quantum of debt and cash flow situation. As a result, free cash flow was not good enough to meet both cost and tenor, as the forecasted cash flow went awry as the aging goal post changed. It was mayhem with banks at your throat to collect debts; businesses reeling under severe cash flow crunches heralded a company with healthy revenues and profits facing major challenges.

Having learned this while facing business turbulence headwinds, I worked on ring-fencing my business with specific vital pledges as one of many of my lifelong learning lessons. Align business growth against given resources and restrict your debt within prudent norms at not more than 2.5 times the company EBITDA as a prudent measure. I now ensure that all my business working capital is paid out from the cost of sales, thereby ensuring minimum profit margins against each contract. This should be allocated toward the cost of financing with factoring in all collectable receivables. I also advise keeping a close eye on DSO—days sales outstanding—not letting that go beyond one hundred days.

3.12.3. PRUDENT CASH FLOW MANAGEMENT IS AN ABSOLUTE BUSINESS NECESSITY

Business sustainability needs prudent cash flow management and cannot undermine this over profits. Overzealousness on the part of entrepreneurs often leads to taking on businesses with a poor payment track record or slow payments, often stacking the interaction with doubtful debts. These also commit to capital costs or developmental costs against the future business that often leads to a cash flow deficit. Businesses need to maintain free cash flow not less than the minimum monthly spend of three months.

Finance should undertake the role of a custodian of risk management and governance.

Risk management is often misconstrued by some in context to controls, but it empowers businesses to mitigate risks and concentrate on growth and profit generation. Therefore, the role of finance is to provide management information reports based on transparent and accurate reporting and help business owners in their decision-making through their reviews and interventions. For instance, the role of finance in context to budget management is a common bone of contention with business owners, and many view it with distrust. This perception is misplaced because a budget is a "sacred" document for any robust business, and finance must act as the custodian.

Compliances, governance, and statutory needs are business continuity essentials, and it is the finance department that has to stand guard over these, especially if others fail to take cognizance. In a case of irregularity or impending business disaster, finance is the last fort to fall and must always emerge as the "savior of last resort."

Reflection Points

- Business prudence matters above all, as the enterprise core business is to uphold principles of sense, where business needs to be profitable and healthy to meet the expectations of all its stakeholders.

- Finance has to map out the commercial risks and, by doing so, help operations to predict outcomes that the business functions want to achieve, not just spell doom and gloom.

3.13. To Build Lean Organizations, We Need a Shared Services Consolidation

Entrepreneurs love the concept of a *lean* organization. The idea of lean is not about big or small businesses. It makes much greater sense in businesses with low margins and inherent risks of price fluctuations with tight cash flow. Lean has now assumed a much finer dimension, with businesses worldwide adopting it as a management tool to achieve cost optimizations with lean structures and related costs.

In my specific case, I wanted to run a business as a pyramid organization where the corporate office was with the group CEO and finance, with HR sitting with support services in a lateral structure, and operations as a vertical with their downstream organization. The idea was to have them independent of each other and consolidate all support functions of finance, HR, technology, supply chain, and customer relationship management (CRM) support functions.

The objective was that, besides the ease gained through a robust shared services platform, business scalability would help reduce the cost of services. At EFS, my current company, I was able to bring down my cost by almost 10 percent in overhead, which came as a massive bonanza in just five years. This came in very handy in a business vertical with a free fall in margins and severe cash flow pressures.

The consolidation of business operations used by multiple operating entities was the ideal solution in the backdrop of evolving market conditions, both being cost efficient, as these eliminated redundancies.

These shared services need to fundamentally include shared accountability of results by the unit from where the work is migrated to the provider. On the other hand, the provider needs to ensure that the agreed outcomes are delivered based on defined measures (KPIs, cost, quality, etc.).

The concept of shared services works well, provided the services offered are efficient, have timely resolutions, and give value-added benefits. The quality needs to transcend beyond routine levels for it to work smoothly.

During the previous years, more and more organizations have adopted this concept with an eye on service consolidation and cost purges. However, shared services have expanded their reach and impact with the advent of new technology platforms. Corporate organizations don't need to rethink their benefits with cloud technologies, CRM solutions, and shared telephony platforms.

At EFS, we realized this opportunity and saw that we could scale many of our shared services by virtue of its captive scale. Within a short period of consolidation, we offered these services to our internal organizations and third parties. This required both innovative thinking and a transformative organization with technology in place to withhold its true value proposition. In five years, EFS is proud to have built very robust shared services with over a dozen services such as finance, HR, supply chain, technology, CAFM, command center, L&D, transportation, staff accommodation services, and store operations, among others.

Reflection Points

- The positive impact of shared services is mostly echoed in financial statements with low SG&A costs and high project margins.

- This makes projects lean enough to maneuver tactically and brings considerable benefits of cost and quality of service to projects.

- Upon reaching a critical mass, shared services can also become a source of revenue by offering these services to third parties.

3.14. A Human Resources Organization Has a Paramount Role in the Overall Organizational Results

In the history of enterprise evolution, the role of human resources has been under scrutiny, and it has been undergoing a continuous churning. Undoubtedly, being a people-centric function, it needs to work in line with how the world is changing. So from personnel to human resources to HR business partners, it has evolved.

In my own professional life, I have seen the role of human resources transforming. I remember in my first job appointment the process was brief. Résumé submission, attending the interview, and reviewing the appointment letter was a short process, unlike the comprehensive checks and balances put in place now, ranging from panel interviews to psychometric assessments to onboarding. However, the process and measures now put in place are indeed the right way forward and are necessary to onboard the right talent.

In those days of the late eighties, I remember that our interaction with HR was minimal. We would seldom contact HR, other than for the routine salary or leave issues. Since then, it has been revolutionized with much more detailed and comprehensive reviews and engagements. I would say it is now much more holistic and people-centric than transactional.

At EFS, we as a service organization recognized that a fundamental consideration for our organization was the fact that people held the center stage. We therefore put our HR department at the forefront of our company, as we long ago realized its paramount importance.

Being centered around employees and their satisfaction and overall well-being mattered whether it had to do with the actual work itself, the work site, or the accommodations they were living in. I realized this at very early stages and then started to work on the fundamentals. First, I revisited the values that strengthen the culture along with HR structures by ensuring that all elements from talent acquisition to employee relations and engagement to progression and retention were mapped.

Then I reviewed policies based on people, and the best standard to embed ethical values, statutory requirements, and business focus. Systems, in terms of the right choice of technologies and procedures, and processes in tandem with the needs of businesses were customized to ensure complete fairness on both sides. It was a herculean task, as the state of affairs in HR regarding mindsets and organizational preparedness needed a transformative shift to be able to support the organization to sync with change. The mission of people first was the ultimate goal.

We kickstarted this in early 2012, and it took us years to achieve certain key milestones. We were able to do that because we were able to rope in all stakeholders with a shared vision toward people being our primary asset and looked at how to nurture that asset through sensitivity and respect at every level of the organization, especially the underprivileged workforce of the organization.

I have never seen such a paradigm shift in organizational overall performance than after rolling out this mission. We increased employee satisfaction levels up to the high nineties and productivity levels in just three years, resulting in spectacular financial results between then and now. Apart from the organization's meteoric rise in overall results with compound annual growth of 17 percent in the last decade and profits in double digits, its HR credentials are implacable. Holding employee retention at 90 percent, with vital employee engagements and initiatives that won awards over the past five years, is itself a showcase of what good HR practices and initiatives can deliver. These credentials demonstrate how the HR role has raised the company brand equity of being an essential business partner.

Reflection Points

- Ensuring staff happiness and welfare through continuous engagement initiatives across various levels, as well as motivation through development and progression opportunities, was our goal.

- We achieved this goal with robust and effective governance of policies, procedures, and systems along with HR service delivery by bringing in the concept of HR service assurance.

3.15. Entrepreneurs Must Rise Up to Manage Their Procurement Processes

Every business stakeholder needs to understand the procurement function's role in any enterprise. Traditionally, the procurement function's primary role is to ensure that all the raw materials, equipment, industrial consumables, and services required for its core business are available. This has now assumed much more vital importance, emerging as an essential tool in profitability and business continuity, and its impact in context to both of these is hugely significant.

In building a robust enterprise, organizing the needed resources remains a critical capability that is a must-have. These all require an efficient hand on resource mobilization, be it people, technology, infrastructure, or materials. In context to people, it is the function of human resources, and for capital funding needs it is finance. However, for the remainder of resources, the onus lies on the supply chain, which must assume the primary responsibility in building any robust organization with diverse needs.

The postpandemic supply chain turmoil has highlighted the key considerations that companies must have in their procurement strategies. Pricing, timing, agility, and flexibility have become critical factors to reckon with. Most refer to the procurement function as apt pricing and timely availability, but this requires much more than these. Timely availability with flexible specs and quantity and assured price range is a business continuity need. No company can sustain steep price fluctuations, long waits, or undesired specs. Therefore, the agility of suppliers matters. The lean and agility paradigms rule the procurement function. For lean, the market winner is cost, whereas in the case of agility the winner is availability. Agile supply chains are required to be market sensitive and hence nimble. This encourages lean (efficient) supply upstream and agile (effective) supply downstream, thus bringing together the best of both paradigms.

Recent global shipping and production challenges leading to supply chain chaos serve as a stark reminder of why these must do more to boost their procurement organizations. In the most recent example, procurements should build a balance between local and international sourcing to dilute the risks of supply chain disruptions and maintain a minimum availability of supplies to assure business continuity. This is an example of how procurement can protect businesses from market pressure on pricing and supplies of commodities and materials without interruption.

Reflection Points

- An effective procurement in this day and age has to rely on technology, as it has the responsibility to analyze data and methods to predict and improve its delivery of products and services to its customers.

- Technology and process-based best practices now rule its functions.

3.16. As a Business, Here's Why You Need to Focus on Yourself (and Not on Your Competition)

If you put in more effort and do your best to give your brand a unique service offering, you can do a much better job handling competition and also achieving solid customer retention.

As per the dictionary by Merriam-Webster, the definition of competition is "the effort of two or more parties acting independently to secure the business of a third party by offering the most favorable terms." As such, for those of you who engage in competition, it can prove to be rather advantageous, as, ideally, this challenge helps you to make your offering more innovative, efficient, and/or durable. It also ensures that the customer pays for your offering's intrinsic cost while also securing value for money.

Competition thus seems normal in essence, but is it worrisome, and does it warrant taking negative actions to get the upper hand? After all, fear of competition is a common factor among businesses around the world, often being embedded as a key point in their strategic plans. But while competition may well be a factor to reckon with, it must not be a source of fear for businesses either.

Business strategies are formulated based on foresight with many facets to consider. Economic forecasts, market trends, labor and commodity markets, government regulations, technology, and competition play roles. These businesses have to devise resilient strategies where confidence, not fear, rules. Any negativity, be it competition risk or market transformation, should be factored in advance and relevant changes made to manage it, instead of devising defensive posturing.

Wisdom demands that businesses must rise *above* the competition, not rise *against* it. Fear of competition or stalking competition is not the right approach, and it is outdated. A company must focus on its internal improvements, leverage its strengths, and introspect on learnings of the past. It also requires exploring new ground, innovating and transforming to stand out, and giving the best customer experience possible. While competition case studies may help, one must not find themselves overwhelmed with competition syndrome.

Preparedness for a business's proper sustenance requires envisioning and planning and a careful consideration of all factors. This includes organizing resources and people to execute plans and managing the aspects to run the business in a robust mode. But often, the company and the people operating it go astray in following the competition, with their overzealous pursuit of the same goal resulting in many failures. Past and present market situations tell this story; be it in COLA or in telecom, the list is endless, with no apparent benefits in sight for most. These misadventures have cost them dearly, and they have mostly been counterproductive.

Competition should ideally be a positive force where each party can learn from failures and successes, but these need much scrutiny. However, many times competition is used as a source of business benchmarking by factoring in select indicators, instead of comprehensive reviews such as turnover, class, size, history, business category, industry, and others. One must learn to draw exact parameters before any comparative exercise is undertaken to conclude with credible competition data in order to try to determine why one company is better than the others.

I personally tend to give a very low priority to the competition risk, especially as I see people reacting very negatively to competition, either with aggression, fear, or defense. I find these fears unfounded and unnecessary. There should be no fear from competition unless you are in a business with limited market reach or if you are simply too small a player in a domain where market forces are pushing for consolidation. Even in such a situation, using innovation and transformation is the way. Prudent businesses need to map their strengths, weaknesses, opportunities, and threats with a SWOT analysis and build a resilient model based on industry best practices.

At the end of the day, one needs to learn how to handle competition: do not fight it, and do not ignore it. Give the client their desired value, which is not money alone but rather a holistic offering. Build your value proposition and stand out. Tell your story and add more personality to your brand. It should be engaging and impactful and also trigger an emotional response to bond with your company over the others. Above all, care for your customers and make client retention, not just acquisition, as the cornerstone of your business development strategy. It shouldn't be all about profits; you should also care about customer retention, because without the loyalty of your customers the business won't be sustainable.

> At the end of the day, one needs to learn how to handle competition: do not fight it, and do not ignore it.

More and more companies are trying to highlight the importance of creating strong customer-brand relationships, because you have to establish some form of trust if you want customers to stay loyal to your brand. Once you start working toward learning more about your customer profile and their needs and, above all, pricing, you will also be able to provide optimized value. If you want to stand out and defeat your competitors, meeting your clients' needs is pertinent above all—aim to provide value for money with the focus being on meeting or exceeding standards and offering quality services, as opposed to only adjusting prices.

In my current role as CEO, my organization has more than 95 percent customer retention while also maintaining a 20 percent compounded annual growth over one decade. We achieved this, as we knew how focusing on strategies would create stronger bonds with our clients, and we made this our core competitive advantage. We also knew that stagnation has an adverse impact. To avoid this, we embarked on a continuous transformation that has helped to deliver a unique experience and resulted in positive feedback from our clients.

Reflection Points

- There's always going to be someone with a better product or service. How do you address this reality in the marketplace?

- If you put in more effort and do your best to give your brand a unique service offering, you can do a much better job handling competition and achieving solid customer retention.

CONCLUSION: READY TO BUILD RESILIENCE?

In writing the conclusion of my book, my most significant challenge was how to conclude the detailed description of my life learnings in a summarized version, where I wanted to highlight the key takeaways for people to connect with my contentions.

The book is a pure, organic version of my real-life journey. Certain events and experiences significantly shaped my thought processes and helped me articulate my management style, shaping my transformation and the successes many people believe I have achieved.

The book has covered the various facets of my life, citing instances of achieving definitive results in my relentless pursuit of driving impact from my actions. I have gone into great detail to emphasize how good values can help build a genuinely sustainable character in business. My book has repeatedly touched on certain aspects of my character attributes that helped in my life to rise against the crises that all businesses must face sooner or later. These are the most potent drivers of a resilient fortitude, whether it had to do with my self-discipline or unrelenting faith in value-driven dealings. Notwithstanding business or people, these paved my way to move forward against all challenges and to chart the success of the organization.

> Certain events and experiences significantly shaped my thought processes and helped me articulate my management style, shaping my transformation and the successes many people believe I have achieved.

The book has covered specific events and instances of how I was able to build a people-first organization and has given examples of how CEOs can apply my learnings for their organizations.

It is my sincerest wish that the experiences I have offered to my readers will make a difference in their lives and the lives of their employees.

ACKNOWLEDGMENTS

The process of writing this book started a long time ago, and this was inspired by many. However, the idea of writing came to me from a friend, Bikram Vohra, who pushed me to begin a column for the *Khaleej Times*. I thank him for believing in me, as I would not be here now if it was not for his assurance.

However, my two daughters, Nyla and Nada, who never lost an opportunity to inspire their dad with the best compliments, also persuaded me to write this book. These two young souls are accomplished professionals whose individual perspectives of the world convinced me to write down my profound experiences, my encounters in life, and my brushes with disasters, which over time made me a man of resilience. Their belief and persuasion led me to finally get into an *author's mode*. Ultimately, I will fail if I don't again thank my wife, Lovita. She has been a woman of substance and with humility in abundance. Her influence further emboldened me to measure all of my accomplishments against the benchmark of the impact they made on others.

In addition to my family, my wife, and two daughters, I dedicate this to my extended family, the people who call themselves "EFSians." These are self-motivated individuals who are driven to live a life of good values. They are people of passion who have created a huge impact at the workplace and for society overall. They have supported me in every juncture of my life at EFS. With their support and openness to change, I was able to steer the company forward. Most importantly, the shared vision we have built as a team at EFS keeps me going. Be it market disruptions, insane timelines on massive projects, or a global pandemic, the long-term vision of EFS and of the team is what *kept us going*.

I would also like to acknowledge my loyal readers. Over the years, these people have resonated with my thought leadership and have given their continuous feedback. They are professionals and entrepreneurs from all walks of life and are at different points in their journeys. A few have achieved their dreams; some are yet aspiring, and some are still struggling to come to terms with a taste of success. Inspired by their curiosity, questions, and feedback, this book includes snippets from years of very honest and candid reflections shared with others. It is meant to shed light on those issues that lie beneath the surface in business, to dispel myths, and to understand the basics of business and life itself in a simple manner.

If there is one gift I can give to the world, it would be to guide and alert people to the challenges they may face by recounting my own experiences and some of the tools they can use to navigate them.

I must name specific individuals who have been an important part of my life, be it my sufferings, happiness, or hectic lifestyle. The head of this team is Charmin, who lives through all my daily highs and lows. Calm and composure are her biggest strengths. She is supported by Anil, who keeps all my travel seamless as part of my jet-setter life. And Taher, my work buddy, with whom my relationship is bonded by trust, respect, and mutual admiration. And finally Aliya, a serious-minded soul with an ever-ready willingness to assist.

Also, I must mention Ghulam, my thirty-year-long partner on wheels, who is my chauffeur, and Nisha, the household help who keeps my home in professional order, from medications to wardrobe to travel bags, all in the perfect place.

Finally, to my extended family and friends, Tarun, Bingo, and Khurshid, who have all influenced me in their own ways.

To conclude, I acknowledge the credit due to all EFSians, and especially the blue-collar workforce with whom I learned to understand the need for insight and compassion.

ABOUT THE AUTHOR

Tariq Chauhan is an accomplished business leader who has been widely recognized for his work in different industries during the past thirty years. Tariq has led some of the most prestigious ventures in banking, transaction services, technology, and real estate in the region, all considered transformative and revolutionary for their time. In his current role as the Group CEO of EFS Facilities Services Group, he has transformed EFS in less than a decade from a $100 million company to a billion-dollar company, which is now an international powerhouse in integrated facilities management (IFM) operating in twenty-one countries in the Middle East, Africa, and South Asia region. He is a seasoned professional entrepreneur, widely respected and globally recognized for establishing EFS as *the* international premium facilities management (FM) brand.

Tariq is a Harvard alumnus with over thirty years' experience in profitable business ventures, including an impressive portfolio of acquisitions to his credit. He has gained substantial business foresight and insights at various levels from his past experience at global multinational banks and his proven track record in building small-to-medium enterprises (SMEs) in information technology (IT), transaction services, and structured and trade finance services.

Tariq has addressed critical topics such as challenges in the global FM industry, diversity and inclusion, community, and welfare of the blue-collar workforce and young leadership as he steers speeches, seminars, presentations, and panel discussions amid high-network individuals, industry veterans, and business schools. For more than two decades, he has delivered a holistic impact through interviews, white paper articles, industry editorials, and speaking engagements to combined audiences of not less than 150,000 people annually.

As a columnist for mainstream local dailies and publications such as *Forbes Middle East* and *Entrepreneur,* Tariq has authored one-hundred-plus published articles on multiple topics ranging from leadership, people, workplace, and business prudence. Tariq has a large following of readers who seek his deep insights.

Tariq stands among the top five CEOs featured in the *Forbes Top Indian Leaders of 2019,* is ranked twelfth among the top sixty professionals in the Middle East by *Construction Business News,* and was awarded the Industry Leader of the Year 2020 by Innovation in Construction and Facilities Management Awards. Tariq Chauhan was listed among the top fifty Indian executives in *Forbes Middle East* for the past five years and also in the top one hundred in *Forbes Middle East* list of top CEOs and executives (2021, 2022). He has set new benchmarks in facilities management through quality service delivery, people initiatives, and innovation.